Roswitha

Memories of a Life's Journey

by

Roswitha Ingrid Scharf-Dessureault

D0965416

Printed and bound in Canada by Art Bookbindery
www.artbookbindery.com

ISBN 978-0-9784628-0-2

To My Dudele Tanisha, and My Princess Aria with my deepest love.

Your Oma Roswitha.

TABLE OF CONTENTS

Acknowledgements

I am deeply grateful for the forty years of my life in Canada and for the so many wonderful friends I have made along my way. They have given me their love and encouragement, supported me when times were difficult, and cheered me along in all my successes. There are too many people to name, but I love them all and thank them from the bottom of my heart.

For the last several years, I have been writing my life story. I attended the Life Writing classes at the Charleswood Seniors' Centre for a couple of years, and my classmates were a wonderful help, encouraging me when I wanted to quit, and giving me advice and suggestions. My thanks to all of them.

In 2005-06 I attended a course at the St. James Seniors' Community Centre called *Write Your Life Story*. I cannot tell you how grateful I am to my teacher and mentor, Ms. Sherry Bailey. The support she gave in listening to me, understanding what I wanted to say, and showing me how to focus my writing was outstanding!

I thank my editor Carolyn Hample for keeping me motivated, for listening, encouraging and never doubting that I would publish this book. I thank Judy Lehn for her constant encouragement, Kay Jakisch for her honest assessments, and my husband Camille, whom I constantly challenge for words. I thank him for his patience and love.

Finally, I want to express my love for this country and all its diverse people, and especially my love for Winnipeg, which has been my home for many years and the scene of my greatest success. I am grateful and proud to be a Canadian.

FOREWORD:

LOOKING FORWARD, LOOKING BACK

Now there is a new chapter in my life. And it is time to write my journey.

For many years now I have been wanting to write something of my life's journeys for my children, Sonja, Volker and Canadian-born Ilona, as well as for my two Canadian grandchildren, Tanisha and Aria. It is hard to do, to find simple words to tell about all the difficulties and hardships in my way. It is also hard to express the deep passion and love of life that have shaped my path. I hope my story helps them to understand where their mother/ grandmother comes from, and what has guided her through her life. Especially Tanisha and Aria should know about my life in Germany during and after the Second World War, and about the struggles and hardships our family had getting settled in Canada. I hope my tale will inspire them in their own lives, and show them that overcoming life's difficulties needs courage, perseverance, and especially faith; faith in themselves, faith in other people, faith that the world will show them the way if they keep their eyes and their hearts open.

So I sit here on a wonderful summer evening in 2005, surrounded by the beautiful plants and flowers, hanging baskets and strawberry beds of our lovely little garden, and gaze at the two bicycles that my husband Camille and I love so much. We joined a seniors' cycling club a few summers ago, and it has given me some of the most enjoyable times I ever had in my whole life. We have cycled all around the city, exploring many different parks and trails, and for the first time I could remember, I felt free of the heavy responsibilities and hardships of my life.

The best time with the cycling club so far was our five-day trip from Winnipeg to Walker, Minnesota, and back. Nineteen of us went, and we had a great time. We started early on a Monday morning and drove the six hours to Walker by car. After a relaxing afternoon and evening in the hotel, we got up early again and cycled for 74.5 kilometers along a "Rail-to-Trail" converted railway line. We could not have had a better day. The sun shone bright, the air was fresh and clear, and the birds were singing. We passed through green forest and smelled the wonderful smells of the trees.

The second day was a disappointment as it rained, and there wasn't much to do, but the next day again was bright and sunny. What a delight! This time we rode the Heartland Trail, another old rail line. All we could hear were the birds and the sounds of our bikes. It was like heaven. We stopped for rests and food and water, but we rode hard! We cycled 98.5 kilometers that day, and all I could think when I got off my bike was: "Oh my sore bum". It is pretty funny that our cycle group is called the Leisure Club when we work so hard.

Now as I sit in our garden, I think about how I am starting a new chapter, a new journey in my life, towards old age and how that will be. But at the same time, I look back over that life and what I learned and what I have accomplished. I think about my little bike trips and how free they make me feel, and how different they are from all the long hard journeys that I took in my life, all around Germany, then across Europe and the Atlantic Ocean to Canada, then back and forth across Canada with some trips to Germany before finally coming to settle for good in Winnipeg. I think about what I learned on those journeys, and how many difficulties and responsibilities I had. And the question is "what next?"

All my life I have worked hard, first when I was a little girl in Germany after the war to help support my family and then to look after myself. After I married Johann and had Sonja and Volker, I worked most weeks sixty to seventy hours at all kinds of jobs and at caring for my children and home. Life in Canada was more of the same, but even harder, because Johann and I had no family here to help us, and our third child, Ilona, was born. Everything was also made harder by the fact that we moved around so much, from job to job and from city to city. When we finally settled in Winnipeg, I managed a busy restaurant, Basil's, and then bought and ran The Tea Cozy, which was very successful. But even then, though the children were growing and becoming independent, I was still working sixty and seventy-hour weeks. I was getting so tired!

After I sold my restaurant in 2002, I thought I would rest then. But after about four months I had enough of sitting around. Not doing things and not being busy, busy, busy, felt wrong. So I took a part-time job at a seniors' home. It was more hard work, but it also was a place that opened my eyes and spirit to what might be ahead of me in my coming life. The elderly people were mostly in their seventies and eighties, and many were in their nineties. Lots of them stayed as active and lively as they could. One beautiful old lady was one hundred years old, and had a remarkable mind and lively personality. But many others were being overcome by their problems. Some had to use walkers to get around, and some needed wheelchairs. Many of them were deaf, and would forget to change the batteries in their hearing aids so they didn't hear what was happening and got upset. Or they would turn the hearing aids up so loud the screeching made the hair on your arms stand up.

Because of the residents' many disabilities, it was hard to really make friends with most of them. But it made me feel good to look after them, and to receive their smiles and thanks when I helped them. At the same time, the work was starting to get me down. I did not like the way the home was being managed, but also I knew that all these old people, even the ones in pretty good shape, wouldn't be getting any better. So, although I was sorry to leave the residents, I quit the job. It made me depressed to think of being stuck with a walker or confused and forgetful. I thought, I would like to be like the hundred year-old lady, alert and happy. But what to do now?

Luckily, Camille and I discovered the cycling club, and it gave me a whole new way to look at things. So, after our trip to Walker, I decided to work part-time teaching German in a *Kinderschule*, or nursery school. The children are between three and five years old, and after the seniors' home they have so much life and light! They are wonderful; so innocent and honest and loveable. This seems a much better place for me to be, and I am still working there. And to my great joy, my Princess, my Aria, has been coming there. Also for the last couple of summers after *Kinderschule* is over, I have been working as a tour guide for Fehr-Way Tours, so my journeys aren't over yet!

So I sit in my garden and all these events -- retiring, the old folks' home, the cycling group, the *Kinderschule* and the tour buses -- make me think hard about my life, and make me even more determined to write about it. It seems important especially to record this because no one else from my family settled in Canada. I hope it will tell the children something about where they came from and about why they are who they are. I hope they will learn from my experiences and have an easier time of it than me. And I want them to know and remember me and how much I love them and how proud I am of them.

PART ONE: GERMANY

1

WAR AND WANDERING

My journey begins in Köln-Lindenthal (Cologne), not far from the Rhine River, in the early hours of September 21, 1940, the second year of World War II. My mother told me that the air raid sirens went off again the night I was born. I don't remember if she told me bombs fell nearby, but my life sure started with a bang! My parents, Mathilde Walter and Heinrich Fiedler, had married in December 1939, but I was my mother's third child. My brother Horst was born in 1935 and my sister Ingeborg in 1937. I think both were born out of wedlock and by different fathers. I never knew Ingeborg until many years later, because my mother had to put her into a *Kinderheim* or orphanage. "Mutti" (mother) never talked about her past life, so I don't know why she had to give my sister away. When my father married my mother, he gave Horst his name, "Fiedler", but not to Ingeborg. Perhaps she was already in the orphanage by then. She had my mother's maiden name, "Walter".

I recollect very little of my early years, except that my father was a soldier and went away to war. My sister Monika was born on January 16, 1942, but I was too young to remember that event. But my fifth year began in uprooting and terror. In 1944, my mother moved us to Darmstadt and my parents divorced on March 29 of that year. On June 8th my mother married another man, but she kept this marriage a secret, and we never knew about it until many years later.

Wedding Day, December 15th 1939, Mathilde with Heinrich Fiedler

Darmstadt, which is about midway between Frankfurt in the north and Mannheim in the south, became a target for allied bombings. Darmstadt was a university town with not much heavy industry. There was no military reason to bomb it. But the Allies, partly because of earlier German raids on British cities, had adopted a policy of deliberately bombing non-industrial German towns and cities to kill and injure civilians and do as much damage to their cities as possible. There were three minor raids between September 23-24, 1943 and August 24-25, 1944. Then, on the night of September 11-12, just ten days before my fourth birthday, there was a huge raid, the worst of the whole war. When the air-raid sirens went off, my mother took us, Horst, me and Monika, to a bunker that was being used as an air-raid shelter. By the time we got there, there was nowhere left to sit down, but a kind person gave up his seat just under the window and we crouched there as the bombs exploded around us. Then there was a terrible huge explosion, and a horrible smell of gas. A bomb must have hit a gas line in the shelter.

Even before the bomb hit, people were very scared and their faces showed their terror. Everyone was sitting very close to one another. After the explosion, there was a moment of silence, then we could hear screaming and crying and roaring noises. Then everything became totally silent until the window above us broke, and a soldier yelled to see if anyone was left alive. My mother lifted us out, and then helped an elderly woman and her grandchild get out. The soldiers put us all in an open truck and took us to hospital. Only one other person besides the four of us, the elderly woman, survived, out of about five hundred in the shelter. We would have died too, except for that kind person who gave up his seat, and for those brave soldiers.

The raid caused a firestorm in the centre and other parts of the city. Where the firestorm was, everything was destroyed. About eighty percent of the city was flattened, over twelve thousand people died, and nearly seventy thousand, including my family, were homeless.

I remember my mother's frightened and teary face as we were put onto the truck. She was probably in shock, and must have been scared we would get separated. Sitting tight together and holding each other on the open deck of the truck, we heard the sirens from fire trucks and the sound of raging fires all around us. I saw the flames and the ruins and I smelled the awful smoke. I remember that we all were in deep shock. Lost and wounded people were trying to find help. There is a story my brother told us: In front of the *Lange Ludwig*, a famous monument in the heart of Darmstadt, there was a beautiful fountain before the bombing. The monument still stood after the bombing, and my brother saw a father running towards the fountain to save his burning son, but there was no water anymore in the fountain. Horst told me he could never forget that image he saw of the burning boy and his frantic father as our truck drove by to take us to the hospital.

I had nightmares later in my life about the little girl who was rescued with me. She had dark hair and soft white skin. She lay at the foot of my bed and asked the nun looking after us for water. But before the nun could come back, I saw the little girl looking at me and then suddenly she turned her head and she died. This and other images from that night haunted me for years. But I think Mutti knew we had to get on with living, and no one talked about the bombing later on.

In the turmoil and confusion after the raid, we had to move around a lot in Darmstadt to find safe shelter. Mutti finally found a place for us in a bombed-out house close to the train station. We stayed in that ruined house for quite a while. Meantime, my father had been declared dead in 1945, so our mother had to support us as best she could. To get money for food she used to go to the train station to sell the watches and jewelry she had managed to hang onto, because many soldiers were coming and going by train now that the war was over, and they were looking for souvenirs or presents for their loved ones. Here she met Leo, a Romanian national and civilian who had been working in Germany. Eventually he came to live with us.

My stepfather wanted to return home to Romania, and take Mutti and us with him. We would travel across what later became Czechoslovakia, across Hungary to Bucharest, and then northwest to Jasi, Leo's home town. So sometime in early 1946 we travelled from Darmstadt with many other people from Hungary and Romania. All of us were refugees looking for peace and a new life.

Because so much had been destroyed by the war, the only way we could travel was in boxcars. Each car had twenty or thirty people in it, and the floors were covered with straw. The boxcars seemed pretty crowded as we all lived crammed together. It was not very comfortable to live in a boxcar, because the only toilet was a pail and everyone used it. I've tried to remember what we ate and how we got it, but I can't.

I do remember that once when the train stopped we could see American soldiers with machine guns patrolling the railroad. We children had been told not to get off the train when it stopped, but I was a very curious child, so I climbed down before anybody could stop me. To my surprise, a nice young soldier smiled and waved me over. He lifted me onto his shoulder and carried me to a table. Then he opened a metal box and gave me his food to eat. I remember I ate everything in the box because I was so hungry. Then he picked some stones up off the ground and we played games with them. A little later he took me back to the train and that was the last I saw of him. But I have never forgotten his gentle, smiling face or his kindness to me.

Horst had also got off the train, but he hid underneath it and explored between the tracks. He said he found a boxcar full of grain that was leaking a bit, so he punched a bigger hole and brought back grain for all of us. He told me years later that we would have starved if he had not found the grain, but I don't know about that.

Wedding Day, July 12th 1946
Donauwörth, Mathilde and Leo
Feraru

We arrived in the city of Budapest, but the Hungarians would not let us go on to Romania. They said we three children and our mother had to go back to Germany, because she and Leo had not been legally married and they did not

19

```
Trp.Nr. 211                    F r i e d b e r g
Name:          Vorname:      Alter: M  F  K  Kl  Beruf:            Wgg.

Fororaru       Leon          43 a  1                Autoschl.,Feinmech.
   "           Mathilde      34 a     1             o.D.
Fiedler        Horst         11          1
   "           Roswitha      6           1
   "           Monika        4           1
```

A u f s t e l l u n g
----

des Trp.Nr.211 v.29.12.46 (Volksdeutsche aus Rumänien und Ungarn)
                    über Piding.

In Augsburg eingelangt am 21.12.46 . . . .   530 Personen
          Privat-Reisende   13   "
          UNRRA-Betreute   8   "
          Regierungs-Auffanglager   652   "

                                                         1.003 Personen

A u f t e i l u n g (abtransport 14.1.47):
                                                  Trp. UNRRA RAL

In den Landkreis Friedberg . . . . . . 209 Pers. 197   -   12
 "   "   "   Nördlingen 157   "   120   -   37
 "   "   "   Dillingen 18   "   5   -   13
 "   "   "   Donauwörth 28   "   -   2   26
 "   "   "   Krumbach 25   "   -   1   24
 "   "   "   Füssen 23   "   -   1   22
 "   "   "   Günzburg 40   "   -   -   40
 "   "   "   Illertissen   5   "   -   -   5
 "   "   "   Kaufbeuren 57   "   -   -   57
 "   "   "   Kempten 75   "   -   -   75
 "   "   "   Memmingen 62   "   -   -   62
 "   "   "   Mindelheim 36   "   -   -   36
 "   "   "   Neuburg 34   "   -   -   29
 "   "   "   Neu Ulm 22   "   -   -   25
 "   "   "   Markt-Oberdorf 25   "   -   -   20
 "   "   "   Sonthofen 20   "   -   -   14
 "   "   "   Schwabmünchen 14   "   -   -   21
 "   "   "   Wertingen 21   "   -   4   78
                 Augsburg-Stadt 82   "   -   -   29
                 Augsburg-Land 29   "   982 P
                                        ----------- ---   --   ---
                                        982 Pers.   322   8   652
                 in andere Regierungsbezirke . . . .   21 P

                                                               1.003 P
```

December 29.1946
(Aufstellung) Transport Number 211 Friedberg
```

want Germans in their country. The Hungarians told Leo he could either go back to Germany with the German woman and her brats or we could stay and all be shot. They gave him three minutes to think about it. At least that's what Mutti told me, and I think it is true. So we returned to eastern Germany, exhausted and half-starved. (Germany was not officially divided by the Allies and the Soviet Union into West Germany and East Germany until 1949.)

On July 12th, 1946, Leo married my mother. But this caused them more trouble later on. So soon after the War, people strongly disapproved of German women marrying foreigners and it was also against the law, so my mother lost her German citizenship. And that was not the end of it, although we children did not learn of it until I applied for her death certificate in 1991. Because of Mutti's secret marriage in 1944, her marriage to Leo was not legal. They had to wait until that marriage was dissolved, which it was March 11th, 1948, and Leo and Mutti remarried on March 27th. Many of the other refugees who travelled with us were displaced persons who had lived and worked in Germany, like Leo. There were Romanians, Hungarians and other middle-European nationalities. These people wanted to return to their homelands but were turned back in Budapest like us. I don't know why. They couldn't all have been illegally married!

Along with many of these other refugees, we then were sent back to western Germany in Boxcar Transport Number 211, which carried 1003 people. In my research at the archive in Augsburg, Germany, I found out about Transport 211 and about my family's travels on it. The Transport left from Budapest, Hungary for Piding, a small town close to the Austrian border, where we were all registered as refugees and given identity cards. From Piding the Transport went on to Freilassing-Bad Reichenhall, and ended up in Augsburg on December 28th, 1946. I remember that I wore an old coat and that all the people in our boxcar were crowded together, I assume to keep warm. There was a little stove in the boxcar, but it did not give much heat, so we had to huddle around it. We were poorly dressed, poorly fed, and cold, always cold.

From Augsburg we were all sent to a refugee camp (*Flüchtlingslager*) at Friedberg, where we arrived on December 29th, 1946. After being in Friedberg for a while, our family and some of the others were moved to a small town in Bavaria called Stäzling near Augsburg, where we lived in a little house. Other families went from the camp to other towns and cities in the region. There I started my grade one schooling. The photo on the cover is of me at school when I was seven years old.

The only way Horst and I could get to the school and back home again was to walk a long way through a forest of tall, old pines, and often I was afraid. I was scared partly because the forest was so dark because of the trees. They stood close to each other and the sound of the wind in their branches was eerie. Many times also I had to go alone without my brother, and this was even more frightening. I was sure that someone would be hiding behind the trees ready to grab me. My stepfather sometimes followed after my brother and me on the way to the school, and when he caught up with us, he would take Horst and beat him, who knows for what. I would hear Horst crying as my stepfather beat him, and that was the most frightening thing of all. But Horst and I had some good times in that forest. He taught me how to find mushrooms, like chanterelles, on our way home from school, and we would take them home for the family to eat.

Even though I was only seven years old, I had to work very hard. When I got home from school I had to wash clothes and look after my new-born brother Peter, who had been born in Friedberg on June 6th, 1947. There was no time to play because once housework was done then there was homework for school.

On January 14th, 1947, we got moved from our small house in Stäzling to another refugee camp in Donauwörth, run by the United Nations. I don't know why we had to leave our little house for the camp, but it seems there was no choice. The city of Donauwörth I don't know much about, only that it is in Bavaria and the River Danube flows by where the camp was built, so the children from the camp went very often in the summertime for swimming. That was fun, but there wasn't much else about the camp that was fun. While we were there, my stepfather and mother had two more children, Aurel and Florel. That meant more work, especially for Mutti and me. I spent more than five years of my young life there, from ages six to twelve, and there I discovered my strong survival instinct, which I soon learned to trust.

Donauwörth
Monika five years old and Roswitha six

Life in the refugee camps was mostly a misery, sad and full of discomfort and hard work. At first there were no cooking facilities in the individual buildings, just only one kitchen for everybody, where each family went to pick up their portion for lunch or dinner. There was a school in the camp, and the girls had to go after school to the barracks' kitchen to peel potatoes. The food was rationed for all families and it wasn't very tasty. Later on, though, we had a stove in our barrack that burned coal and wood, so the mothers could cook food for their families.

Other than peeling potatoes afterward, I have almost no memory of what the school was like. Only one incident stands out. All the school children were put on a truck and taken to big potato fields. There we had to go down on our knees and pick the ugly brown potato bugs off the plants and put them into tin containers. There were thousands of them! We returned to school and showed each other how many we had in our tin cans of those crawling, ugly bugs. That was fun. I think we received a couple of pennies from the school for picking the bugs, but I don't know what we would have spent it on.

Every Sunday we had to go to church. My stepfather changed his religion very often; he was then Greek Orthodox. Everybody wore their Sunday clothes, even though we were all very poor. One Sunday before Florel was born, my first two half-brothers were baptized along with some other children. There was a big old bathtub instead of a font, and we watched as the priest baptized first Peter and then Aurel. Peter was about three years old and he did not like being baptized, I can tell you. He yelled and cried and I shrieked out of fear for him. Then came baby Aurel, and he didn't like it any better than Peter. He cried even louder. I think the water must have been too cold and it frightened the children. After the ceremony the parents had a small celebration with neighbours and friends.

But there wasn't much besides school and church, except for hard work, hunger and crowded barracks. I think there were about ten or fifteen barracks in the camp, and in each barrack there were three or four families, each with anything from two to six children. In our barrack there were four steel bunk beds where two children slept up and two down. The parents were separated from the children with some curtains that were made out of green and brown army blankets.

Often there were fights in the camp, especially among the men. A big problem for the men was that they were angry and frustrated because there was no work for them and they could not support their families, so anything could turn into an argument or a fight. Sometimes it started with the men playing cards; other times it was arguments with their wives, or fathers and mothers hitting their kids, or kids fighting with each other. Sometimes it felt like everybody in that whole camp hated everybody else. The fact that the men could get hold of alcohol, I don't know how, just made everything more explosive. One time we saw a man stabbed from behind because he wasn't playing cards right. Was he cheating? I don't know. He stumbled and then fell to the ground. I don't know what happened to him after because nobody would talk about it. Another time, we watched as a man who had stripped his wife dragged her outside naked and began beating her. She cried and screamed, but nobody tried to stop him. In those days you never interfered between a man and his family, and lots of men beat their wives, and children too. And I think the people who just stood and watched were maybe afraid they'd end up in a fight too if they did anything. You must understand also that this camp was occupied by different nationalities and so often one could hear from different barracks arguing, shouting and tempers flying out of control, but it was in all different languages, so it was hard to understand what was happening. Maybe the other people thought the person getting beat up had done something to deserve it; who knows? It was terrifying for us to watch that kind of thing when we were so young, and

I don't think any of us ever forgot it. But kids are tough and I don't imagine things were any worse in Donauwörth than other camps. And I got tough too. I minded my own business and tried not to get in anyone's way and just kept on with my life. I went to school, I went to church, I did my work, and we played when we could. But one time I did not get out of the way in time.

On Christmas Eve, 1949, when I was nine years old, there was a fight between one of the neighbours, a Hungarian man, and my Romanian stepfather. The men hated each other and so often they started fighting. That neighbor was a nasty person but Papa's hot temper was also part of the problem. Papa was not very friendly, and the Hungarian disliked him because Papa wouldn't drink with him or spend time with him. They fought mostly about their countries. Each one believed his country was the best, and the other man's no good. On this particular day there was a lot of commotion going on and Horst and Monika and I ran out of the barrack to see what was happening. When we saw them fighting, we were going to run and get the camp police, but we did not get very far.

Mutti was then pregnant with Florel, and she came out also to try and stop the fight. We screamed for her to get back into the barrack. She did, and Monika and Horst made it back inside too, and papa quit fighting to make sure Mutti got back into the barrack. But I did not get away in time. I

Donauwörth
Roswitha nine years old

26

Picture of the *Flüchtlingslager* Donauwörth 1946

slipped on the last steps to the house and fell right into the icy-cold snow, and I lay there stunned. That Hungarian had a broomstick and when he saw me lying on the ground he started hitting me! Perhaps he was so full of rage that he did not realize or did not care that he was hitting a child. Or maybe he thought that beating me was a good way to hurt Papa. I was terrified and screaming and crying and hurting but nobody could or would make him stop. Finally he stopped hitting me and went home. Or maybe he saw Papa coming back out with a very fierce expression on his face. I think Papa would like to have killed that Hungarian, but instead he put me on a sled and as fast as he could he got me to the hospital in the camp for treatment for my injuries. Like the man who beat his naked wife, nothing happened to the Hungarian because of what he did. They just moved his family to a different barrack and so life went on. The incident spoiled our Christmas, though, that's for sure! And for a time afterward I was almost too frightened to leave the barrack, then I put it all out of my mind. But I have scars from that beating, not only physical but emotional also. In fact I only remembered it years later when a doctor asked about the scars I have on my body.

Once we got the stove, Mutti could cook meals for us. I loved her *pflaumenkuchen* (plum cake) and her *rot kohl* (red cabbage) and dumplings. But we only had these special dishes at Christmas or other important occasions. I learned many of her recipes and cooked them many times over the years. There was one dish that I have never cooked, though, and hope I never will. Mutti would take left-over stale bread, and roast it with onions and spices, and then she would add water to make a soup. We ate a lot of bread soup in the camp.

In the summer, many of the women made themselves gardens behind the barracks, where they planted vegetables to supplement the camp rations, and also grew a variety of beautiful flowers. They also had little shacks with benches where they could have some quiet time and sit and talk with each other. We children loved to be in the gardens playing and picking flowers.

We had no toys and no dolls. But we always found a way to play. Our toys were stones off the ground. Maybe that G.I. who played with me by the railway track taught me that, or maybe kids just play with whatever they have. We became very imaginative with those stones. They became many things in our imaginations. I would use four or five to build a house, and a stone of different colour would become the family in the house. I also learned how to count using stones. I always searched for unusual stones with my friends. We would count them and exchange stones with each other. I remember my sister Monika and I often played checkers with the stones on a "board" we scratched in the dirt. We made another game with a great big tree that grew in front of our barrack. It had long, flexible branches, and it bloomed beautifully in the springtime, with white flowers. After all the flowers had fallen from it, we would grab onto the long branches and use them as swings to see how high we could fly. We laughed a lot and had great fun around that tree.

The feelings of the girls in the camp for each other were of great importance and comfort; that I remember very vividly. Unlike a lot of the men, we learned very early to get along with each other whatever country we had come from, and so at an early age I learned nondiscrimination. I consider that as one important factor in my life, and it was certainly good preparation for my future in Canada, where people from all over the world have had to learn to live together. We would gather in small groups and talk about the camp or what our lives might be like if we weren't there, or what would happen to us when we were older. And we made up games with what was at hand.

One game the girls had was to pick flowers from the

many little gardens and put them together in all their colours and varieties to make beautiful flower crowns. Often we sang songs and shared our flower crowns with each other and dreamed we were princesses. We also played with the flowers by pulling off the leaves and exploring the inside of the petals. Then we would stick the colourful leaves against the window. The daylight would shine through them like church windows. The sweet smells and beautiful colours of the flowers helped us forget for a bit the dreariness of the camp.

I had one girlfriend in particular. Her name was Theresa and she was Hungarian. We shared our family stories with each other and often we cried together. My family left Donauwörth in 1952 and I never saw her again, but I never forgot her name. And I always remembered our dreams of being princesses. On my fiftieth birthday, I created a flower crown for my wedding to my second husband, Camille, and fulfilled my childhood make-believe.

By the time I was ten years old, Mutti had her sixth baby, Florel, and I became responsible for him as well as for Peter, who was four years old, and Aurel, who was one year. There was no time to play. I had to learn early what work meant and I became a very serious young woman, even though by years I was still a little girl.

One nice thing happened when I was nine. Mutti made for me a doll out of old, striped material and socks. The doll's face was stitched from old wool. She had a brown body and her arms dangled down because they were a little longer than her body. Her eyes were beautiful, and I played with her a lot. I can't remember, though, if I ever gave her a name.

There was some excitement, too, besides the fights all the time. In 1950 the Danube River had a very bad flood. The water broke its banks and the whole camp was flooded. We all had to be evacuated, so they used small boats to get us out. Everyone ended up in the school gym, where we had to sleep on the floor. So many people in one place! The children thought it was great, and we had a lot of fun running around. We were too young to know how serious the situation was. It turns out the Danube flood was only one of many historic floods in 1950, including the one in Winnipeg that older people still talk about.

I had beautiful, curly long brown hair, and many people admired it. Most of the time I wore it in two pigtails. I also was a little plump as a young girl, as you can see by my school picture. When I was eleven, my beautiful pigtails attracted a young Romanian man, who got to know us. He and my step-father were countrymen and he became Aurel's Godfather.

One Sunday, when Monika could not go with me to church, the young man told my parents that he would take me there on his bike, because he knew that I liked cycling. My parents trusted him, so they sent me off with him. But we never ended up in the church. Instead, he took me to a park where he asked me to play with him. He did things to me that should never happen to a young girl, things that were very painful and frightened me very badly. Then he warned me never to tell a soul about what had happened. His warning was almost as terrifying as what he had done to me. Even now the experience is incredibly painful to recall, and very hard to write about. My body and soul are appalled by those experiences.

I knew in my bones that what he had done was wrong, but I was too ashamed and too scared to tell anyone. After the first time he was always wanting to take me to church. I fought with my parents about going with him, but I was too afraid to tell them why I didn't want to go, so they never understood, but kept making me go. My parents had so many worries, maybe they never noticed that my behavior was changed. I was no longer that happy-go-lucky girl I had been. I was always afraid to go outside to play alone, because that man lived right next door to us. He also often visited my stepfather in our home. Then he would pat me on my shoulder and wink at me as I ducked my head in shame and walked away. This went on for two years and was the end of my childhood happiness. I can't write more about that time. It makes me still sick today when I think about it. I was too young to have to learn about that kind of fear and pain, but it made me determined that I would not let what happened to me destroy me, so in the end it made even more fierce my determination to survive.

2

FIGHTING BACK

When I was twelve years old, in 1952, a cousin of my mother's came from Darmstadt to Donauwörth to visit us. She said she could help us get out of the refugee camp and back to Mutti's home town after eight years away. I only remembered Darmstadt as all bombed, but now she told us that the city was slowly rebuilding and we would return home. That was the best news I ever had in my young life. After so many years living in turmoil and fear, my excitement ran high, and I could not get fast enough away from the camp and that horrible Romanian man. My only grief was saying farewell to my best friend, Theresa. We went one last time to pick flowers in the gardens, and we both cried so hard and hugged each other so tight it hurt. We had been so close and had shared so much. But I did not even tell Theresa what that Romanian man did to me.

Life was a little better in Darmstadt. The city was being slowly rebuilt to the point that people could live there again, but many parts of the city were still in ruins, and the city officials placed homeless families wherever they could find shelter for them. Our first home was in a basement of a bombed-out house on the Adelungen Strasse. The place was very dark. We slept on mattresses on the floor and we had an old stove there where Mutti cooked, and that made it a little better place. But we had to carry the water from a well upstairs down to the basement. It was not pleasant and we still were hungry many times. I think if you have been really hungry many times you never forget. How could you?

Monika and I had our first Communion in Darmstadt in 1953. Mutti was still a member of the Roman Catholic Church, and wanted us confirmed in her faith. We wore white lace dresses with white socks and shoes, and daisy flower crowns on our heads. In our hands we each carried a very big white candle. The candle also was surrounded with white lace. The white signified that my sister and I and all the other girls having our first communion were pure. After what had happened to me! I didn't feel very pure, but there was nothing I could do except pray that God would forgive me.

My parents must have made sacrifices to dress us so nicely. But then Mutti had always tried her very best to dress us respectably, even though we had so little money. She would say "we are poor but the outside world does not need to know; we all will walk with our heads held high with pride." It seemed so important to her. She had a song that she often sang. It goes like this: "*Immer nur Lächeln und immer vergnügt/ doch wie es darinnen/ ausschaut, geht niemanten/ was an.*" It means "always smiling, always smiling, how it looks in our inside, no one needs to know." It is from an operetta that was one of her very favorites, *The Land of Smiles,* by Franz Lehar.

Once we were settled, we started school again. I was thirteen by now. I loved going to school in Darmstadt. It was the first time that I experienced a nice teacher that I could remember, and she gave me good marks. I loved knitting and cooking and had always "A" in those subjects. But she knew that we were poor. In spite of Mutti's best efforts, Monika and I had to wear aprons to school so we would not dirty our only weekday dresses. Not all the poor girls wore aprons, but if you did, you stood out. My sister and I felt often ashamed to wear the aprons, because we were pushed around by some of the other children and it was difficult to make friends. So I showed my strength in sport, like hurdles and long-jumping and hand-ball tossing. Because I was athletic, I eventually became accepted in the school by the other students. But it was hard to keep up in school. As soon as classes were over, I had to go to work and often I could not finish my homework. Fortunately the teacher was very understanding and kind, and I think she really liked me. I am so sorry I do not remember her name, but I do remember her gentle face, surrounded by her beautiful straight brown hair. She was about fifty years old.

My first job was in a shoe factory on the assembly line for two or three hours after school, where I got trained to sew pieces for the new shoes. The money helped support our family. I had to push thick leather under the sewing machine needle, then sew leather soles piece by piece for the shoes. There were many sewing machines, rows of them, and behind each one a woman to operate it. The supervisor would walk up and down the aisle to oversee our work. We had to do a certain number of those soles each hour we were there, and we were paid by the sole. The supervisor was quite a harsh man and would scream if we made a mistake. Or sometimes he would throw the soles at us or he would smack us on our ears with them. Every one worked very hard to not make any mistake, and very fast to make money. I did that job for one year, but the work was too hard for me. After a while my hands hurt from the work, making it hard to write in school, so I decided to search for another after-school job. I found one in a carton factory where I stapled cartons together on a big pedal-operated machine. There I folded heavy brown cardboard into boxes and then stapled the corners together. I had to watch out not to get the staples in my fingers. I liked that job because many jolly women worked there, and there was a lot of laughter which made the time pass quickly. But it was still physically demanding, and interfered with my schooling.

Papa did not get any steady work and he was not a happy man. He tried to find peace in different faiths, but he never could. He did not drink but he had a bad temper, and often he would hit us with such force that we would go to school with bruises. He made us all very fearful of him. Sometimes he would take the belt out of his pants, then fold the belt in two and swing it. The person who was the closest received the blow. It was especially horrible when he beat our mother. I remember him leaning over her one day with a small hand-saw, hitting her over the head with it. She bled so badly that she needed stitches in her head. Papa was also very hard on Horst. He received the most punishment of any of us, and it hurt him dreadfully that he couldn't stop Papa from beating Mutti. When Horst was sixteen, he couldn't take any more, so he left home. He sent us money he earned, but he never lived with us ever again.

I think my step-father's violence was partly, maybe mostly, because of his helplessness and frustration. He was trained as an auto-mechanic. There had been no work in the camp, and now that he was getting too old, and his German was too poor, it was even worse. Mutti tried to help him with the language, but she was not successful. Also, seeing his step-son earn money for the family when he could not must have been terrible for him. It was the father's job to support the family. So he took his rage and frustration out on us. The more angry and frustrated he became, the more we were afraid of him. I do not remember him being violent with us in the camp, but my brother tells me different and I do remember how he would beat Horst in the forest when we lived in Stazling.

There were some nice times with my stepfather. He wasn't angry all the time. He would play his Romanian music and be in such a good mood, and then he gave us hugs and kisses and would be very loving. I loved Papa when he was like this, and it is hard to believe that he could change into such a very different person. But I feared him more than I loved him. In spite of everything, I think Mutti also loved him in her way. He had been a very tall and handsome man when she met him, and he had done his best to try and look after her and her children even before he had his own with her.

Sometimes my step-father defended me from other kids who picked on me when I was playing outside, and he was always very pleased when I came home from school with good marks. He had very warm brown eyes and dark skin. It could be that he was a gypsy, but that I was not able to find out. He did one thing that really made me think he had some gypsy in him, though. He would take books and put them under the table legs to balance the rickety table, and we all had to sit around the table and hold hands. Mostly at these times he spoke Romanian, but he explained to us what he was doing in his broken German and so we understood to be quiet. What questions he asked "the spirits" I don't know. If the table tipped towards one of us, then he said it meant that bad things would happen. It could be to our family or to just one of us. That is what he told us. Sometimes he used the Bible under one of the table legs, hoping that it would stop bad things from happening to us.

The only thing we had to do was hold hands and bow our heads. Then we would wait to see if the table moved. Sometimes, one of us would push the table top gently with our hands so he would not see who did it, and then we would break out in laughter. This made him very angry, and his eyes would turn to black pearls and his face would become dark red. We did not try that too often. Even though we joked about it, his gypsy table frightened me, because it made me think of ghosts and other weird things. I had a very vivid imagination.

Horst and I still saw each other even after he left home. We went often on Saturdays to pick the wild blue cornflowers

37

from the corn fields around the city. Then we bundled them together and sold them at the market. That was our first adventure as young business people. Oh, we loved it! My brother became my teacher and my best friend as we worked together, and today I am still his little sister.

At some point Horst began to work in a cookie factory. Now that was something! I wanted to go there too and my brother arranged that I could work there after school. That meant that I could leave the carton factory. At the cookie factory, I looked after the owner's dog, a German shepherd. That dog sure liked me. The owner's wife taught me how to cook the dog's favorite food: beef bones and oatmeal. Ugh! I can still remember the awful smell it made when I was cooking it.

After we had lived in the basement for some time, our family received the good news that we could move into the small house next door This house was also partly bombed, but the front of it was livable. We had for the first time running water and a bathroom, also a new stove and three bedrooms. This was the first time we children had so much room to ourselves. It was exciting to share a room with just my sister Monika, and the three boys shared another room. We loved the space and freedom so much we ran back and forth through the rooms, until finally there were some doors put between them.

From the street through the entrance on the left side of our new home on Adelungen Strasse was another bombed-out apartment building and we played in the ruins. We were the only children around so we made our own fun, and we thought that this was fun because we did not know how dangerous it was. We jumped from one stone to the next or we ran up and down the bombed-out staircases. That building was about six stories high, and when we jumped around, bricks would sometimes fall. We would laugh because we thought it was exciting. We never thought that maybe a brick or a beam might fall on our heads, or part of the stairs fall down while we were running up and down them. Mutti didn't like us playing there. I can still hear her voice, saying, "Get down from there right now before you get hurt!" but we didn't listen.

Many things changed for the better the year I was fourteen. First, we had the best home we had ever lived in, and finally Papa found a religion that gave him a more positive outlook on life when he converted from Greek Orthodox to Jehovah's Witness. The Witnesses did not have a regular church. They met in a big hall where on Sunday Papa would take us to listen to their message. The children from all the different families would sit in the front rows, and often the elders gave us pennies for ice cream to make sure that we came back. We thought that was o.k. Mutti never complained about Papa taking us there instead of the Catholic church, and sometimes she even came with us to keep peace in our home.

But Papa's new religion did not make him happy for very long, and soon our visits to the big hall ended. No more pennies for ice cream. Soon he found yet another religion, and started to take us to a different church. This time it was a Mormon temple. I never knew what he was searching for in all these religions. Maybe he didn't either. Whatever it was, I don't think he ever found it.

In 1954, two years after we moved back to Darmstadt, out of nowhere came a new sister. It was Ingeborg, the daughter Mutti had given up sixteen years earlier. This is the first time we knew about her, and what my mother had had to do. She looked a bit like me. She was plump, and had the same brown hair. But she was not very tall, only about five feet. She was very shy, but sweet, and was very helpful in our home. She was still living in a home with other children, but Mutti would not answer very many of our questions about why Ingeborg was there. I didn't know if she had come with us meaning to live in our home or if she was only on a visit, but she stayed with us only for a short while and then she was gone again. I don't remember much else about her visit besides her name and her face and her sweet temper, though, because I was having my own teenage turmoils.

Finally, in 2004, fifty years later and after many years looking for her, I found my half-sister again. I felt very happy, because I had always wanted to know what happened to her, and where she was, and how she was. When I received the news from Germany that she was found, I almost fainted and tears ran down my face like rain. But the news also brought great sadness, because before I found her, Ingeborg had had a stroke, and could not speak with me. Instead, her son Lorenz was the person who answered my letters. My contact was exciting and I sent pictures of my family, but after a while her son did not want to continue our correspondence. He told me it was upsetting his mother too much because it made her

Roswitha, "Mutti", and Monika, Darmstadt 1956

40

remember very bad times in her life. I am sad about this, and sad that she was never a part of our family, but I hope that I can meet her once in my life time. For now I respect her wishes to be left alone.

The best thing about 1954 was my fourteenth birthday. I received a wonderful present! I remembered how excited I was by it not long ago, as I was watching my fourteen year old granddaughter, Tanisha. She was coming into the gym at Minnetonka School with all the other kids. They were carrying their musical instruments for the school concert. Tanisha played the recorder. As I was sitting in the audience waiting for the music to begin, my thoughts were swept back to that special birthday. I had received a beautiful red accordion and I loved it so much. I was learning to play it, but I didn't have it very long. Once again, there was not enough money coming into the house, so my beloved Instrument was sold for food. I was so sad then, but I did not argue with my parents, I accepted that it had to be, that food was more important than music.

Years later in Winnipeg when I celebrated my forty-fifth birthday I had another special surprise. My three children were there, and Horst was visiting from Germany. The celebration took place in a Korean restaurant, Tokyo Joe's. My family was excited when I came in, and they all kept looking at me with big smiles on their faces. I wondered what they were up to. Then I noticed a big box on my chair and every one said, "Open it! Open it!" I wanted to wait, but Horst said, "Nah, open it now!" So I did, and what a wonder! In the box was a beautiful red accordion. My family all applauded and all the memories of my fourteenth birthday and my joy when I opened that first accordion flooded back to me, and it made this birthday even happier than before. It brought tears to my eyes. It seemed they all knew my childhood story. Now they all asked me "Play! Play!" I was a little embarrassed, but anyway I took that instrument and tried to press some notes out of it. No notes came, only a funny squeak, and every one laughed and laughed with me. I said, "Now, I really should learn to play this instrument."

Music is for me the essence of life. I love to listen to all kinds: Greek, Latin-American, jazz, classical and operettas. As I said, Mutti loved Franz Lehar who wrote *The Land of Smiles* and we learned about Beethoven and Schubert. When I was sixteen years old I briefly joined the Franz Schubert choir. It was such pleasure singing there. When we were still young my brothers and Monika and I listened to *Peter and the Wolf* by Tchaikovsky. We were fascinated by the music and the story, and by the way the different instruments were used for the different characters. Horst also loved Mozart and Chopin, and taught me to love them too.

In the 'fifties and 'sixties, music was played in the parks of many German cities and it was very popular. My family went often to the Herrengarten in Darmstadt. It is a beautiful park with small water fountains and a lot of flowers, like Assiniboine Park. Music was played there every Sunday morning. There we listened to brass bands and march music. We loved it! We listened very carefully to the music and sometimes we would tap with our fingers or wave our hands gently and pretend we were the conductor. It would make me feel like dancing, but only the very small children would do that. Music has continued to be very central to my life. My first husband was even a musician. He played in many bands, and especially he loved jazz.

But back to when I was fourteen. It was a very full year. First my sister Ingeborg came home, and then I got my red accordion, and then I lost it. And then another thing happened. Mutti and Papa were called to the Darmstadt Courthouse about a man who had sexually abused some girls at Donauwörth in the refugee camp. Of course it was that horrible Romanian. I was not his only victim, and now my shameful secret was out. I had to go myself to the

Courthouse to make a statement, in front of a judge and two police officers. I was scared, and ashamed, and when I was called to testify, everything that man had done to me came flooding back. It was so awful. All I could do was cry. But my stepfather became enraged. He was not angry at his countryman, because he did not believe the man would have done such things to me. He was angry at me! He started to hit me, and he threw me on the floor and kicked me with his boots right in front of the policemen! He had to be restrained by them. Even after we left the Courthouse I was still so frightened that he would beat me some more. But now my own mother started to hit me! She kept slapping my face on one cheek and then the other cheek until they burned, and she called me awful names and said I brought shame on the family. I could not believe that my own mother would think I was lying about such an awful thing and would be so hurtful. I started to turn against them at that point and to think about when I could leave them, because they were so cruel to me.

After all the court business was over, even though my stepfather and mother hurt me very much, I was a bit relieved. I was going on fifteen, and hadn't seen that Romanian since I was twelve. I hoped I would never ever see him again. But my wish was not to be. After the Romanian served his jail time, he came back to visit. I was devastated that my stepfather would allow this man to come back into our home after all that he had done. To be so insensitive and ignorant as to believe that if anything happened it was all my fault and I was only that bad girl who caused the family so much shame! But he even more believed that nothing had happened and that I lied about his countryman to get him in trouble. After he behaved like that, my stepfather was almost as repulsive to me as the Romanian.

After that was the first time that I ran away from home. I went to my brother at the cookie factory. I don't know how long I stayed, but finally Mutti came to see me. I remember she cried and told me that the bad guy had gone and I could come home. At least she believed he had abused me. And when I came home, nobody ever spoke about it again.

A while later, our family moved to the Kiesstrasse into a four-bedroom apartment. It was in an eight-story block and a lot of children lived there. It was a great new neighborhood with a much better school. And I began to be interested in boys, which my parents did not like very much. My first charming young man was called Peter. He was eighteen years old and he was a handsome, tall young fellow. I had my eye on him, I can tell you! I flirted with him a little bit, and to my surprise he invited me out to a movie. I was very excited. It was the first time I would go out with a boy. I dressed up in a beautiful blue velvet dress that had a white collar and a pocket on each side of the skirt. I felt like a princess. He came to pick me up, and I stepped out of our apartment to greet him. How handsome he looked! But my mother did not like the look of him; it could be that she remembered what had happened to me in Donauwörth, or maybe she just thought he was too old for me, so she sent him away, and my wonderful evening was ruined.

But what did I know about young men? What did I even know about Peter? I was very angry and humiliated. What must Peter think of me now? But now that I have two daughters and two granddaughters I can see why she did it. Then, to top it all off, Mutti sent me to the room I shared with Monika to clean up the mess I had made getting ready for my "wonderful evening!"

In 1955 Mutti received from the German Government some money for the loss of her soldier-husband, my real father, and her home in Köln Lindenthal. (Cologne was an important target for the Allies during the war, and air-raids began in 1942.) That Christmas was one of my happiest ones. Mutti made a traditional German Christmas for all of us. She cooked the traditional German dishes, beef *Rouladen*, red cabbage, roasted bread crumbs, and mountains of mashed potatoes. She started baking cookies one month before Christmas, and Monika and I helped her. We made vanilla *Hörnchen*, butter cookies, and other treats. Our home was full of wonderful smells and happiness, a real delight.

On Christmas Eve in the afternoon the younger boys had to have their bath. That was another job for us girls. Then Monika and I had to get dressed in our best Sunday clothes. By five p.m. we were called in to the livingroom where there was a Christmas tree all beautifully decorated. Under the tree, there were so many gifts. I had never seen such a pile of presents before. We had to sing songs and recite the poem that we learned for that special Christmas. In the evening we had our dinner, and then we got to look at our Christmas gifts. After that, we attended midnight Mass. My gifts were outstanding. I received a khaki jacket and colourful slacks, not to mention a red three-speed bike! We also got our first black and white TV. I remember it all as clear as yesterday. It all seemed too good to be true. I couldn't wait till spring came to ride that beautiful red bike.

I finished school in 1955 and then I attended what they called in Germany a household school till 1957. I learned about cooking, knitting and bookkeeping and I studied how to take care of babies, though I was already pretty good at that. I had lots of practice on my three half-brothers. In other words, I was taught how to be a good housewife and thought I had been prepared for life.

In the meantime I continued to work and go to school. Every school day at the early hour of six-thirty I went to the cookie factory for a couple of hours to earn money and then I had to run all the way to school. Many times I was late. Then I had housework to do at home, and often had to baby sit my three little brothers. But that was life in those days. Even so, I often was very sad because I could not spend time with other teenagers and make some friends.

One day as I was playing badminton with Horst by the driveway at the cookie factory, a man came and stood at the big entrance door and watched me. This happened a couple of times until my brother asked "who is that man? And what is he doing here?" Horst went and talked to the man, who told him that he was my real father, Heinrich Fiedler. What a shock! I did not know anything about him, not even that he was alive, so at first I could not understand what Horst was telling me.

Mutti had never talked about my real father. He was a mystery to us, even though Horst, Monika and I all carried his last name. But after he came to see me, I asked her about him, and she finally told me. She said she had loved him very much. They had been married on December 15, 1939 in Cologne. But what with the War and him going to the front and not seeing each other, they decided to split up, and they were legally divorced on March 29th, 1944, in Darmstadt. I had many questions. What about my sister Monika, who was born in 1942? I found out that she had a different father. My father's short visit didn't make things better for me. He went away and I never got to talk to him, and then Monika began to resent me. I don't know for sure, but I think she was very sad that she didn't have the same father as me, and that she never knew who her father was because he never came to see her.

I did find out from my Mother that my father could speak a variety of languages and he played the violin and the banjo in a band that he led. The band was called "Beno" and he started it when he was in the army, to escape from serving at the Front. He played at Red Cross socials for the soldiers and at dance evenings, and sometimes he played in the Officers' Mess. He seemed like a pleasant-tempered man who was content with his life, and he had a wonderful sense of humour. I met him once more a few years later in the apartment of my then-future mother-in-law. He came and wanted to talk to me, and he also asked for my sister Monika to come. His visit was very short. He explained to both of us that he was only my father but would like to stay in touch with both of us. He was a slender man, about five feet, eight inches tall, with a very nice smile and a gentle face. He had very short black hair slicked straight back. Shortly after, I remember, he also had a meeting with my mom. But what came out of that meeting I never found out. I never really got to know him but I learned a little bit of his life on his first visit, and more when I met him again years later.

In the summer of 1955, when I was not going to school I worked at a carnival to get away from home. It was a travelling amusement park like the Red River Exhibition, with many attractions. There I sold tickets in an amusement booth for adults and children where they could win stuffed bears or other toy animals if they won the game. There was a rollercoaster and a creepy enclosed booth where you could pay money to see midget people perform, and a snake dancer. There was a dark "ghost ride" where skeletons and cobwebs were hung down from the ceiling to brush you as you went by, and scary figures in weird costumes would pop out to frighten you. There also were rides for the children, little colorful wooden horses on a carousel that had beautiful music playing as it turned and turned. The electric bumper cars were more for the adults and you could hear laughter everywhere. At the music stands there were live performances every hour and people would sit around and listen and be happy for the moment.

There were also ice cream stands, stands where you could buy German sausages, and everywhere you could see colourful balloons. There were so many things to do, lots of fun for the families and the kids. I loved it! I also sold ice cream in a stand. There I earned good money for our family. And I also ate a lot of ice cream, because we did not

47

have that at home. It was free for me, and I ate so much my stomach hurt. I started to dream of running away from home and joining the circus, but that dream never came true. I had so many dreams; but in a poor household only some dreams sometimes come true, and many others never do. I had a beautiful voice and I would have loved to have been a singer, but I didn't think that dream would come true either.

Our home life was not improving. My stepfather became ill and so I saw him only as an angry old man, and more and more often he beat on our mother. This was very upsetting for all of us, especially Monika and me. Sometimes we tried to stop him but that made it worse because he already knew that what he did was wrong. We always were very afraid he would swing at us or hit Mutti even harder, and start to yell and shout as well, so we learned to stand back and be quiet as it happened.

We hated him for hitting her, and it hurt us to see how very sad she often was. She was a very pretty woman, with beautiful black hair. It had grey streaks as she became older. She was slender and graceful and about five feet, six inches tall. Her eyes were hazel and would shine when she was happy. She had such beautiful long fingers one might think she could have been a pianist. Mutti loved dancing when she was a young woman, and always loved to whistle. Often I asked her to whistle for me and she did. I loved my Mutti and I know she loved me and my sister and brothers. She devoted her life to looking after her home and her six children, and she did it on her own. She did not have any help. She had no parents or brothers or sisters to help her, so we had no grandparents or aunts or uncles. So sad, how little I remember about her.

Monika and I also both loved to dance. So when I was sixteen and she was fourteen we often went on weekends to dances at a restaurant and dance bar called *The Crone* in the old city part of Darmstadt. It was fun for us to look at the boys, and we were pretty-looking girls, so the boys flocked around us. But I cannot tell you with what fear we both went home if we stayed out later than we were supposed to. Our step-father would wait up for us, and his belt was our welcome home.

Finally in 1956 a very nice thing happened. On Sundays we were allowed to go to a dancing school named *Boilke* in Darmstadt. It was a very respectable place with a good reputation. Mutti must have saved money and arranged for us to go there, because she knew how much we loved to dance and how much trouble we had if we came home late from our outings. We learned waltzes and tangos and etiquette and so on. Mutti was very pleased to see us go and she was very proud of what good dancers we became.

We had been attending about a year in the dance school when it was arranged that the girls would take their lessons on one side of the room, and the boys would be on the other side. All the parents could come and watch their sons or daughters. The teacher then would pick a partner for everyone so boys and girls could learn to dance together. I especially remember one boy. I did not like him because he had sticking-out ears and red hair, but he liked me, so when we had our exam day to show our parents what we had learned, he came to ask me to dance.

Each couple had to pair up and then dance into the ball room. We were the third couple, and as we entered waltzing, I was so nervous! Then one of my high heels slipped and I fell on to the floor and my yellow dress with a big white petticoat went right over my head! The boy was so embarrassed, and so was I. But he lifted me up and danced with me as if nothing had happened. We won the prize for the English waltz. I was so proud of winning, and proud of the boy who was so quick and kept us dancing. I remember him giving me a small purse as a gift for that evening dance.

3

BREAKING FREE

In March 1958, my sister and I were in an amusement tent in Darmstadt. There was music playing and people dancing around the tables, swinging their beer steins to the "humtata humtata" rhythm. All around was the aroma of cotton-candy and burnt almonds, and the sounds of people enjoying themselves. This was Darmstadt's *Heinerfest*. It is a five-day celebration held every year since 1951 in the centre of the city, around the old castle and in the Herrengarten park which is nearby. It started as a way to encourage the people when they were still rebuilding their city. Now it is the

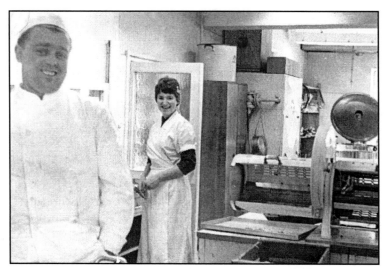

Roswitha 1956
In the Army kitchen

second-largest city fair in Germany.

Music fans had the choice between six live stages and an enormous music program of jazz, swing, and classical music. There was a merry-go-around, a theatre, and many entertainers: jugglers, magicians, belly-dancers and clowns performing around the Luisenplatz under a gigantic tent. There were places for people to dance until midnight, and in the market place one could sit at ease and drink a glass of wine.

There it was that I met Johann, a handsome young man with piercing blue eyes. We started to chat, and soon our conversation was all about music. I had got a job as a helper in a German army kitchen after I finished the household school, and I had been asked to sing in the Officers' Mess. I loved to sing in the army kitchen because the echo was so great, and that is how it came about that I was asked to sing. I told Johann I needed a guitarist. He said he could play the guitar, so that evening we arranged to meet at the Mess.

It was a wonderful evening! I sang modern songs, although I can't remember which ones now, and Johann played the guitar, and from then on we were a couple. I was seventeen and a half years old, and he was my first boyfriend. Johann was also very young, only twenty. His parents had paid for him to become a pastry chef, but his real ambition was to be a musician.

Johann introduced me to his parents. His father was a nice man and good to me. I remember that I often tended to his leg, wounded by a bullet in the First World War. The bullet had hit below his knee and shattered his shin bone. It developed into an ulcer and very often it would begin to weep, and a splinter from his shattered shin bone would make its way to the surface. I would use tweezers and remove the splinter, and then clean the wound. It would heal, and he would have relief from his pain for a while.

Johann"s family had a nice home and I liked them all.

There were only two boys and they were both very spoiled. His mother learned that my home life was a misery, and she was very kind to me. My mother was not so kind to Johann. Mutti and I had a big fight about him. She wanted me to stay away from him. She thought I was too young and she did not like him. She told me that he was not the right man for me. I think she was also unhappy because he was a Lutheran, and we were Catholics. I also think she didn't want me to leave because she loved me very much and was afraid of losing me. I often think about that, that I was her strength because I made her laugh and I helped her always in the home.

But I was madly in love, and life at home was becoming more and more unbearable. So I ran away after one fight with my mother about Johann, I climbed out of the living-room window with what I had on, a dress and my house slippers. I had not thought before that I would leave home. It was a spur of the moment action. I was so upset with Mutti and she with me. I went immediately to Johann's parents' house and told them what happened. I never lived with my parents again except for a little while when my mother was dying. I didn't even see Mutti for three years after I left, until I was married and had my first child.

After I left home, I decided I wanted to become a medical masseur, or what we call in Canada a massage therapist. This was a well-thought-of profession in Europe, although it was not yet popular in Canada, as I would learn. Johann's mother helped to arrange for me to go to a family who owned and operated a clinic in Lampertsheim, a small town about forty-five kilometers away from Darmstadt. It took about an hour by train to go there. The clinic was a husband-and-wife operation. I became their apprentice, and the couple gave me room and board and a very small pay. I had to get up at five in the morning and load the wood and coal into an oven that provided the heat for the sauna. The clinic had about six massage tables, in rooms divided with linen curtains. They had also four bathtubs for special treatments. They trained me over the days and weeks to give massage and how to operate the sauna. The sauna had to be at a very precise temperature to give its full benefits. I also learned about therapeutic baths, like *Fango* therapy. This is where a mass of paraffin wax is put around the patient's body and left for a while. The body starts to sweat and through that the healing process begins. I also learned about *black moor*, where a mass of black earth from the Black Forest is placed onto different parts of the body. It relaxes the patient and is also supposed to have healing powers.

The clinic was very modern for that time, and it was an excellent place to learn, but I often cried and was homesick. I had to stay up late at night to learn from my medical textbooks. My room upstairs in the house was very small, with only a bed, a sink and a small table and chair. I missed Johann very much. He could not come to visit me for six months. I told him how unhappy I was with that family; I did like the work and what I was learning, but the couple were very demanding and I worked for many hours at hard dirty jobs for very little money.

After a year of apprenticeship and a very nice letter of recommendation, I returned to Darmstadt and looked for my own place. I found a small room with a bed and a sink in a family's home. To continue my clinical education, I started working for the Osterbring family, who owned and ran a medical clinic in Darmstadt. The family was wonderful to me and there I stayed for nearly three years to finish my education as a medical masseur.

In 1958 I had to find also a part-time job besides working at the clinic, because Johann and I had decided to get engaged to be married. We had to save money because our families could not help us, so it was that I found a part-time job in the Hotel Lehman. The owner was a single lady, Mrs. Lehman. Her hotel was a *Garni*: it had many rooms and a small restaurant, but the restaurant only served breakfast. The hotel was a very elegant building, eight stories high with black marble stairs, and the owner taught me a lot. For example she would take me to the little restaurant and show me how to do a table setting in an elegant way. She taught me how to serve customers and sometimes she showed me in her home how to dress stylishly. She always was so elegantly dressed. In my eyes she was the most perfect, elegant lady I ever met. She talked to me about the good life and gave me knowledge about good food. Often she would take me with her for shopping and show me different vegetables that in those days I did not know anything about. I was grateful to her for taking me under her wing, and being so good to me. Also I saw for the first time wealth, and that impressed me. So did her independence. Here was a woman on her own and she was a successful business person. Her skill and her knowledge about life encouraged me that I could do anything. She would say "you can be whatever you want to be!"

Here is a little story from one day's work in the hotel. Mrs Lehman asked me to clean her bedroom and so I did. Because she was rich, all her clothes were beautiful. In her bedroom she had lots of mirrors and shelves, and on the shelves there were many wonderful bottles of perfume. There was one particular bottle that attracted my attention, a soft blue crystal bottle, big and round with a crystal stopper. I couldn't resist looking at it. How long I stood there I do not know, but my hands longed to touch that beautiful bottle, and finally I did. Very slowly I lifted the crystal stopper off and I smelled that perfume and put a little on my finger. Oh, what an amazing smell that was! I returned the crystal stopper in a hurry, but the wonderful scent made me feel such a lady. After cleaning up, though, I became very worried. What if Mrs. Lehman could smell the perfume on me? I would get into bad trouble! I thought, "I have to do something quick", so I went to the

55

bathroom and scrubbed and scrubbed my hands in the hope she would not notice. She came later to inspect my work, and she talked to me as if nothing had happened, so I guess she didn't smell anything. Today I can still remember the smell of that perfume. It is called *Diorissimo*, from Christian Dior. Years later, when my second husband Camille and I went to New York on our honeymoon, he gave me a bottle of it. It smelled as wonderful as I remembered.

My favorite memory of Mrs Lehman was what happened on the day of my eighteenth birthday. I came to work and discovered she had set up a wonderful breakfast table and placed a little blue box on it. I asked, "Is that for a customer?" She said no, and to my great surprise she told me to sit down at the table. I didn't want to, because I felt I did not belong there, everything was so elegant. I said, "Oh no, I'm supposed to work." After her telling me to sit down again, I shyly did and she joined me at the table. First we both had the tasty breakfast that she had made. Then she congratulated me on my birthday and asked me to open the little blue box. I cannot tell you how I blushed as I opened the box. There was a blue aquamarine ring in a gold setting! It was the first ring I ever had in my whole life. I put the ring on and to this day I have never taken it off. She told me the aquamarine would give me strength in life. I thought that would be very good luck, because my name, "Roswitha," means "great strength" in Old German. It is the name of a famous nun who lived in the tenth century in Saxony. Mrs. Lehman also gave me much advice about life that I took to heart.

Mrs. Lehman was very kind to me, but she was also very fussy. There was one job that I had to do that I did not like. The hotel had eight flights of black marble stairs, and one of my jobs was to clean them from the top floor to the bottom floor. I had to take black polish and with a brush rub the cream into the marble. She would inspect to see that I got the polish right into the corners of all the stairs. I had to use a toothbrush to do that. After the polish was applied, then I used a brush to shine every step from top to bottom. It was very strenuous work, and took a long time to do, but I always did my best.

Ms. Lehman did not have any children that I knew of, and I think she watched over me like a mother would. She knew some about my hard background. I visited her years later on one of my trips to Germany from Canada, and my admiration was still there for her. And she was so proud and happy to see me and to learn what I had made out of myself. We talked and talked and laughed and cried. It was so good to see her again.

In the meantime, shortly after my birthday, Johann and I got engaged. Mrs. Lehman was not pleased that I would marry Johann, because she thought I was too young and should complete my training. But she told me that it was my choice and did not nag about it. Anyway, I was determined. Johann's parents loved me and I felt safe with Johann and them. I had not visited my mom since the day I had run away, but when she heard that Johann and I were engaged, she sent a lady from the Catholic Church to the little place that I had rented to try to convince me that my young man was not good for me, because he was Lutheran and I was Catholic. I told about the visit to Johann and his mother and she then sent me to a Lutheran minister to take a course of six weeks to learn about Lutheranism and to receive a blessing from the minister.

Why did I go to so much trouble to learn the Lutheran religion? Because I was so much in love with Johann and I know we would get married no matter what. To be honest, I also wanted to be done with my family and everything about their life. Sometimes I have wondered if I should have listened to my mother. I thought about her often because I felt so guilty about the way I left home. But I wouldn't have changed anything because I was in love with Johann.

4

GETTING MARRIED

In early 1960, Johann was called up to the German military. I had saved up money and we went to the Darmstadt City Hall on March 5, 1960, for our license and then to the church and got married. I was very happy, but also a little bit sad on my wedding day because I only had my brother Horst there. No one else from my own family came. I think they knew that I was getting married, at least my sister Monika knew, but I guess they disapproved so much they would not come. Johann's family was there, of course, and Mrs. Lehman. She came to the City Hall and gave me an orchid that I wore on my black suit.

Johann and I had found our own one-room apartment with a little kitchen. We fixed it up very nice, and that room became our bedroom and living room. All that time I continued working at the Osterbring medical clinic. A lot of soccer players came to the clinic and I treated them. They liked the way I looked after them, and so I was asked by the Darmstädter 98 Soccer Club to look after their players as a volunteer masseur. I did that for a full year. I travelled with the team to different tournaments in small towns and if someone got hurt, I ran onto the field and helped them. My Red Cross certificate was very useful for that job. It was a lot of fun. I also continued to work part-time in Mrs. Lehman's hotel until my first child was born in our small home the next year.

The baby was ready to be born at 1:00 a.m. on January

31, 1961. Because she was my first child, I did not really know what the birth would be like. The midwife was an interesting lady, but she was not very sympathetic to first-time mothers, and a bit bold in her speech. I went to her home for training in birthing techniques, and the last time I was there my labor pains began. She took me home, and told me to walk up the stairs to our apartment on the third floor. By the time I arrived upstairs, the baby was ready to come. It was

Roswitha with Sonja, in Darmstadt
1961

such strong pain that I cried out very loud and hard. Well, the midwife just put her hands on her hips and said to me, "When you made this baby inside you, you heard violins. Well, now it's ready to come out like the bass fiddle, and that's all there is to it." She made me laugh, but I was still crying hard. But I have never forgotten those words.

The baby was a big baby. She weighed ten pounds. She came quickly and the doctor had to come to help the midwife stitch me up. Johann was right there with me. He helped the midwife and wiped the sweat from my forehead. When it was over, the midwife wanted coffee but I don't think Johann made any for her because he was more concerned about me and the baby. She was so beautiful! We gave her the name Sonja, a Russian name meaning strength, just as my name, Roswitha, does in German. The midwife left after she knew I was o.k., and Johann left too, to hurry and tell his mom and dad about their new granddaughter. I also asked Johann to inform my mother. She came to see me that very night after not seeing me for three years, and we had a very tearful and loving reunion. She brought me cooked chicken to eat.

We had for Sonja a wonderful baby crib made out of wood, with beautiful white lace curtains. I had taken off work for six months to breast-feed her, hoping I could go on later to finish my examinations for medical masseur, but it was not to be. I had all my training but the certificate was missing. Meantime I continued to work at the Osterbring Clinic as an apprentice. When it was time to go back to work, sometimes Johann's mother would keep Sonja for me, or sometimes I would walk to the clinic pushing her in her baby-carriage. The baby stayed in the family room where I breast-fed her between patients, and the whole family helped look after my child. So I worked there until we moved to Berlin.

On August 31, 1962, my stepfather died. My heart ached for my mother as she only had the three boys left at home, but I did not attend the funeral because Papa had been in a tuberculosis sanatorium, and I was afraid for Sonja. At about the same time, the doctors discovered that Mutti was very sick with colon cancer. She would not be able to look after the boys anymore. Peter was only eleven, Aurel nine, and Florel was seven, so the Catholic Family Service came and took them to a children's home. Johann and I and the baby gave up our nice apartment and moved into my mother's home to help and look after her, after her operation. This was difficult for us, because Mutti needed lots of care and attention, and she was too sick to leave the baby there during the day. So we had to take Sonja to Johann's mother. Johann did not like this arrangement, and I had a lot of arguments with him about it. Finally, we arranged for Mutti to be looked after by the Catholic nuns, and my sister helped her also. She died on October 8, 1962, just before her fiftieth birthday. It was hard to lose my mother, and very hard for my half-brothers to lose both their parents in such a short time.

The boys came from the children's home for the funeral,

and since Peter was an altar boy, he was the one who had to throw the first handful of dirt into Mutti's grave. I remember that I was so sad my throat was all tight, but I could not cry. My sadness was like a tight knot in my heart and I could not let it free. My guilt for running away from home and then not looking after my mom right to the end of her final illness stayed with me for a long time. Horst and Monika came to the funeral but Ingeborg was not there. I don't think she even knew that our mother had died. After the funeral, Peter, Aurel and Florel went back to where they were living, and our family was completely split up.

At the present time, Horst, Monika, Florel and Ingeborg are living with their families in Germany, and Peter with his family in Costa Rica. My heart goes out to my brother Aurel's three children in Germany. He left them behind when he died on October 6, 1999 of the same illness, colon cancer, that our mother had. I loved him very much.

Johann and I moved on with our own family life. We found an apartment and I became pregnant for the second time. I went to the hospital alone on Easter Monday, April 15th, 1963. Johann was stationed at this time with the army in a small town in Germany to finish his two years compulsory training, so he could not be there for the birth. The next day the nurses encouraged me to walk around in the beautiful flower garden that surrounded the hospital to induce my labour, and on April 16, 1963, my son Volker was born at eight twenty-five in the evening. It was very quick. I felt a sharp pain, and my water broke and splashed all over. There was no doctor around, so my baby boy came into the world all on his own. I yelled for the nurse and she came running with a big smile. I was so happy that I had borne a son. He was beautiful, with a head of thick, dark hair. There were six beds in the hospital room and I was the only one with a baby boy. His Mutti. I was a very proud mother, and I was so excited by the birth of my son. But I was also so tired,

Roswitha 1963 Darmstadt
Sonja, two years old and Volker, four months

and I felt so alone without Johann that I cried and cried with happiness and sorrow until the nurse gave me something to calm me down. I stayed in the hospital for five days, and then Johann's mother looked after us.

When Johann finished his compulsory service with the army, he wanted to learn more about music, especially the tenor saxophone, and so he went off to Remscheid to a music school for two months. Remscheid lies past Düsseldorf in North Rhine-Westphalia, 233 kilometers from Darmstadt. I stayed alone with the children and I continued to work at the Osterbring Clinic while Johann's mother looked after the children. After Johann came back from the music school, he played professionally at the dance bar at the Henninger Tower in Frankfurt. His dream was to become a famous musician. He also played some concerts in Frankfurt and in Darmstadt, where he received a lot of good reviews in the newspapers. He was a very musically talented man. But to earn money for our family, he had to go back to his first profession as a pastry chef at the *Konditor*, or pastry shop. He hated that work and often he was unhappy because he could not fulfill his musical dreams. I was content with my life. I adored my two children and I continued to enjoy working with the Osterbrings. But Johann decided we should move to Berlin, and I agreed.

Germany had been divided into West and East Germany after the war in 1949, and in 1961 the Soviets decided to divide Berlin, which was inside East German territory but was open to the west, because too many people were leaving East Germany through Berlin. In August, 1961, they built the Berlin Wall, cutting the city in half and dividing many families. The wall lasted until November, 1989 after the U.S.S.R. collapsed. We began to think about going to Berlin when we heard that Willi Brandt, the mayor of Berlin, had announced that he would help young couples with children from West Germany to come to Berlin. Brandt wanted more West German young people to move there and have families to make sure West Berlin would survive. He said he would help them get settled. A lot of young people went, and that attracted us. Also, Johann's brother Lothar was already there and the musical life was very lively. Berlin was also the city to be in because of the culture, its music, theatre, cafes. So we decided to go.

The Osterbrings gave me a very good letter of recommendation, and I hoped I would find a good job in Berlin. The whole Osterbring family came together to wish me farewell. Many tears flowed and they left me with many hugs and kisses. They told me that anytime I was welcome to their home. I stayed in touch with the family for many years even from Canada. I really loved them. They taught me what a happy family could be and I learned from them so much and we had such good times together in their home. I was like another daughter. When I first went there to work, Mr.

Osterbring thought I would have been a good candidate for his oldest son to marry. but that was not meant to be because I was already with Johann. But as we got ready to move, I was worried if this was the right move for the children. Would we be able to give them a better life in Berlin? Also my Sonja and Volker were safe in Darmstadt with their grandmother and the Osterbrings to help me look after them.

We arrived in Berlin in August, 1963. At first we had a hard time finding a home, so we lived for a while with our children in a bombed-out eight-story apartment building where Lothar was living with a bunch of other musicians and intellectuals and painters. The apartments had been broken up: some were regular apartments with doors and regular rooms; others, like ours, had one big room divided into private spaces with curtains. Because of this, the noise level was really high.

As I said many intellectuals and artists lived there. Johann loved music and playing his saxophone, so he felt quite at home there. But it was not a nice place for children, because the artists and musicians and their girlfriends were hanging around all the time. So we looked and found a nice two bedroom home in Schöneberg, a suburb of Berlin.

In the beginning it was fascinating to be in Berlin. The city was alive! But we were always aware of the wall that surrounded West Berlin and separated it from the rest of Berlin and from East Germany, and we were always aware of the military presence of the Allies. We did not go into East Berlin because I was so afraid of the Soviet and East German soldiers, and scared we would not be able to get back to West Berlin. And when we went to see Checkpoint Charlie, the crossing station to East Berlin, it made me even more frightened. I was not especially politically inclined, but Johann had a better understanding of the political situation and he very often discussed it with Lothar and their friends. But I am very happy to have had the opportunity to live in

Berlin for three years and to have seen the beauty of the city and watched it grow.

But we just also had to go on with our own lives. It was essential that I find a job. Four months after arriving and with two very good letters of recommendation from the clinics in Lampertheim and Darmstadt I got a job at the Auguste Victoria Hospital in Berlin in the Physiotherapeutic Department where I was once again able to use my skills and training.

Roswitha 1964 (right)
Auguste Victoria Hospital, Berlin

In the meantime, our children were being cared for during the work-week by the nuns at a kindergarten. We had to have them there very early in the morning so we could get to work on time, but there they could go back to sleep. It was a very modern daycare for the time. All the children had their own towels with their names on them, and there was a wonderful playground for them when they were outside. We picked the children up at four-thirty at the end of our working day.

Johann worked at a prestigious patisserie in the *Café Willi*

Schmits and on weekend nights he played music. Sometimes on weekends we strolled on the Kurfürsten Dam or we went to a coffee house in the afternoon. We also had the opportunity to go to classical music concerts conducted by Herbert von Karajan, an internationally famous conductor. We took the children to see the animals at the Berlin Zoo, and also to the concerts that were offered right in the Zoo. In the meantime I took an evening course in chiropractic foot care. I was so proud when I received the diploma signed by five doctors. With that diploma I could do foot care at the Hospital Auguste Victoria Krankenhaus Berlin Schöneberg.

We had established ourselves and made wonderful friends in Berlin and our life as a family was coming together, but suddenly things changed again. Johann met a young woman where he worked at the patisserie. He decided that he wanted to leave me, and that he would leave Sonja with me, but take Volker with him to live with this girl. I had the inspiration to invite the young woman into our home to show her our two beautiful children. Johann was in shock when he found out. But she came, and she and I had a very nice time together, except it was painful for me to think that this girl was my husband's lover. As she left, she told me that she would never take my child away from me. Johann and I reconciled and he realized that it would be wrong to leave me with two young children, or to separate the children. I think this is how things were meant to be. I do not belong to any particular religion, but I believe that

Roswitha 1966 Berlin

67

all of nature, our Mother Nature, is alive and that there are spirits or guardians who will help us if we ask for help and follow what our hearts tell us.

We lived in Berlin from 1963 until September 1967. In May of 1967 we saw a documentary film about Canada. I thought, "What a beautiful country!" The families there had such big houses with recreation rooms, and the country was so big! So much space and so inviting! I remember it was an advertising film for new immigrants. I was so impressed and my excitement was so great that I went to the Canadian Immigration Department the next day to ask how to immigrate to Canada. They gave me the papers to take home. Johann was excited to go because he hoped he could continue his music education in North America, maybe at the Berklee School of Music in Boston. He was still dreaming he would become a great jazz musician. We both were so young and the adventure and the challenge were so inviting. Life altogether changed for the better in our marriage as we concentrated on getting ready to move and looked forward to a new life. Oh, we had such big dreams! We filled out all the papers together and, shortly after, we were called to an immigration hearing. By July 1967 we knew that we were accepted into Canada.

The immigration officer gave us vouchers for the train once we got to Canada and Immigration in Berlin also decided where to send us: to Winnipeg, Manitoba. That was their decision and so that became the destination for us. Johann asked about Toronto but the officer advised him that Winnipeg would offer a better life for a family. Johann was at first disappointed. Toronto would have been his first choice, especially in regards to music. But we accepted going to Winnipeg with the thought that when we were once there, then we could move. There was a German-language newspaper at the Immigration Office called *The Canadian Courier* and Johann noticed an advertisement for a pastry chef. He wrote a letter to apply for the job. Not very long after we received news from the bakery that he was accepted.

Immigration booked our trip for September 13, 1967 on the Holland-America Line ship, the *S.S. Maasdam*. The cost for all four of us was fifteen hundred dollars which we had to pay ourselves. We also had to deposit one hundred dollars into the Bank of Canada, a requirement for immigration.

I had no idea where Winnipeg, Manitoba was, so we studied the maps. We sold everything we had and went with five suitcases and a blue trunk on the train from Berlin to Darmstadt on September 2, 1967 to say farewell to the family. We stayed for ten days in Darmstadt. Our children were still very young, and did not have any idea about what great changes were coming into their lives. They accepted all our decisions and were happy as long as Volker could have his *Lego* blocks and Sonja her dolly, her *Schlummerle* (that was a love name for the doll that Grandma had given her). In the children's minds we were off on an adventure. Johann and I were very excited about starting our journey to the new world and a new life for us and the children. We were full of hope for a good life and so our marriage flourished again.

PART TWO: CANADA

5

SAILING TO CANADA

On September 12 we left from the train station in Darmstadt. It was so hard on Johann's parents to say farewell to their son and me and their two grandchildren, and it was hard for us to say goodbye. There were many tears. But they sent us off with good wishes for our new life. They gave us the address of a young Darmstadt couple who had moved to Winnipeg many years before. We did not know them, but it felt good to have a connection in Canada.

I remember waiting at the station with the children on the hard benches for the train to come. We left Darmstadt at two-thirty a.m., and got to Rotterdam at ten a.m. From the train station in Rotterdam, we took a street car and we went to the Wilhelminakade, the huge shipping terminal, and found Holland-America Line's New Pier 40 where the *SS Masdam* was docked. I will never forget when we saw for the first time how big that ship was. It was awesome!

Sonja, Volker and Mom
September 12 1967 Darmstadt at
2:30 a.m. going to Rotterdam

As we stepped on board, immediately we received directions to our cabin. It was number 357 on "A" Deck.

The *S.S Maasdam* sailed on Wednesday, September 13th 1967

Gross Tonnage: 15,024
Passengers: 879
Crew: 308
Length, overall: 503'3"
Breadth: 69'0"
Height to Boat Deck: 68'6"

It was a nice cabin with two bunk beds, a sink, and port-holes where we could see out. The kids right way had fun looking out through the port-holes to see the ocean. Then we went on to the deck to see all the people who were saying farewell from the pier. I held Volker fast by the hand and Johann looked after Sonja. So many people were standing on the deck of the ship and on the pier and there was so much excitement and so much crying and waving! We did not have anyone saying goodbye to us, but we waved to the people on the pier anyway. I knew then that I had left my country and my life in Germany behind, and I cried and wondered what would be.

The *S.S. Maasdam* sailed on Wednesday, September 13. It was our home for eleven days. The captain was J.C. Pothof and the voyage was number 161. At five p.m. on that first day, the ship's huge horn blew and we set out to sea. Once we were at sea, I completely forgot my fears and excitement started to take over. We went around the deck of the ship to explore our new temporary home, a whole city in one ship. There were five hundred and sixty passengers and every nationality on board. We got tickets from the Steward on our deck for the dining room. We sat at tourist-class table number A 23. In the dining rooms there were three sittings at different times for each meal, and what amazing food was served. We could eat what our hearts desired. I saved the menu and it still makes my mouth water.

When we got to the dining room, we discovered that all the tables there had been bolted down so they would not move about if there was a storm with big waves. After we ate, I went with my two children to the library, a wonderful place with plush chairs and elegant wooden tables, and books everywhere. There we looked around for children's books and then we went to the kindergarten that was located on the upper deck of the ship. The kindergarten had very big windows and one could see a great distance across the blue ocean and its big waves. The children could go every day to the kindergarten where they could play and be safe. We parents could then acquaint ourselves with the other passengers and explore the ship. We made friends right way

Sonja, Volker and Mom
Boat Station 9 (left) in the Kindergarten

and I also spent time with our children at the kindergarten.

On the second day at sea there was a mandatory safety exercise. It was announced by seven short signals on the ship's sirens, followed by one long signal of the ship alarm bells. That meant that we had to go with our steward to the lifeboat station and put on our lifejackets. The lifeboat commander gave us further instructions on how to get into our lifeboats. Our boat was number nine. Each lifeboat would take about fifty people, maybe more.

There was much to keep us busy on the ship. On the sun deck there was shuffleboard and we played there with our children. There was also a glass-enclosed promenade with deckchairs where one could lie back in thought and watch the endless sea with its high waves. We had the chance to go to "B" Deck where there was a hospital and physician's consulting room and a photographer's shop. We went one day with the captain onto his bridge to see how he sailed the ship. It was unbelievable! To ensure safety and a successful voyage, the ship was equipped with the most modern navigational and electronic aids that were available at that time to the commander and his navigation officer. You would have to see all those instruments to believe how complicated it all was.

The ship had a smoking lounge with a live band, a movie theater, the library, a post office, a hair salon and a first-class upper deck. As well as the menu from the dining room, I collected the passenger list and *The Ocean Post,* which was put out weekly by United Press International News Service. The newspaper was printed right on board and given to all the passengers. I have copies of the September 13 and September 20 editions of *The Ocean Post.*

After four days, we had high seas and that was scary! The waves came house-high over the ship. Many people became sea-sick, including my family and me, but we eventually got used to the motion. Many times as I walked with my kids on the promenade deck, I could see the endless horizon and sometimes the sun would break though the clouds and sparkle on the sea. How beautiful! Sonja and Volker would want to stand looking over the railing to see the seagulls flying behind the ship and the many other hungry creatures that swim beneath the waves to catch the food thrown out from the kitchen. I was very frightened for the kids even though there were high railings and some had been closed in. So I always held them tight by the hand. And sometimes the sea was so rough and the sky so gray that we could not even go out on deck.

Roswitha
Captain's Ball prize party

The captain and his stewards made elaborate afternoon and evening parties to keep the passengers entertained.

S.S. MAASDAM.

There were many amusing activities, for instance a prize party where we all had to make a hat or some other clothing out of paper. I made an elegant hat out of black and white paper with a very thin wire ring and won a prize. Another time there was the Captain's Ball and this time I made out of paper a joker's costume. Oh that was fun. First I made out of the paper and the thin wire they gave us a three cornered hat, one side black and the other sides white, then I created five paper pompoms, three for the hat and two for the shoes. For the costume I used a tee shirt and stuck on white and black paper with pins. I wore white leotards under my shorts. My slippers were great. I used my shoes wrapped around with paper and stuck the pompoms onto the front. But I needed to walk very carefully in them so the paper didn't tear. Again I won a prize. I still remember as I walked into the dance room with my costume for judging, my children and Johann sitting at a table and laughing out loud. I think they were very happy for me and I was so proud of my own fantasy-designed costume. We had great fun.

Our children were always with us when they were not in kindergarten, and often there was conversation with other immigrants. We sat around in groups and discussed what life in our new country would bring us. I think some people were very anxious about immigrating. They sat many hours in the lounge with their heads in their drinks! The conversations were sometimes very hard because I did not speak or read any English. Johann had to translate everything, even the menu from the dining room. But I did try to learn to speak with my eyes and my hands, and I tried to show my emotions in my expressions.

Our voyage took us by way of Le Havre and Southampton, and past Greenland. The last day before our arrival in Quebec City, on September 21, was my twenty-eighth birthday. It was celebrated at the Captain's dance with our new friends. On the next day, the ship's horn blew to let all of us know that we had entered the St. Lawrence River. We docked in Quebec City harbour, but it was a short stop. A Department of Immigration officer came on board to welcome us and to see our passports. All the passengers who were Canadian citizens stood in one line, the new Immigrants like us were in another line and we all received the stamp in our passports which allowed us to enter Canada. Our family's card number was 138. And then slowly our ship went on from Quebec City. Everyone on board stood outside on the promenade to look as we passed by a big castle. It is called *Le Château Frontenac* and it is a very famous hotel. You could hear the passengers' voices ooing and awing. Again many cried including me, maybe out of joy or out of fear of the unknown, maybe some of both.

As the *S.S. Maasdam* arrived in Montréal on the morning of September 23, everyone we had made friends with said farewell and wished each other good luck. We left the ship full of curiosity to see what was ahead. We felt like real pioneers! But then we had to wait and wait many hours until our five suitcases and one blue trunk were unloaded off of the ship. 1967 was the year that the City of Montreal hosted the 1967 World's Fair, Expo '67. But we did not get a chance to see it. Instead, we took a taxi with the kids and our luggage right to the CPR train station in Montréal. All we had time to do was admire the beautiful station before we departed Montréal late in the afternoon, for the two days on the train to Winnipeg.

We had tickets and vouchers for food and a sleeping compartment on the train that the Immigration Office in Berlin had given us. It was wonderful to sit in the glass dome car and enjoy the incredible scenery in our first experience of Canada. We travelled through many small towns and villages and we saw for the first time some native people who travelled short distances with us on the train to their destinations. The kids enjoyed the train ride. It was a very interesting experience, but the language again became a problem. People spoke only French or English, and I understood neither, although usually I could communicate with people without using words, like on the ship. But there was one instance where my face was red. There were two restrooms on the train, one for men and one for women. Johann went for a smoke and I followed him, but the man in the men's room told me that I couldn't be in that room because it was for men only. Johann had to explain that to me, and I had to go to the women's powder room all alone. I remember how frustrated and humiliated I felt, and I realized the handicap I had not to speak any English.

When we arrived at the CPR train station in Winnipeg with our little belongings, curiosity made us look outside the building towards Main Street, Oh, how poor it looked! The buildings were very run down and there were billboards everywhere. I wondered "Where have we come to? Is this the wild west?" Stories we heard in Germany told about wild horses riding like the wind down the main streets of the towns, but only in my imagination could I see that.

6

SEARCHING

It was a cold day on our arrival. We called the people at the address that we had received in Darmstadt, Ria and Reinhardt Doersam. What wonderful people! We had never met before, but Reinhardt came to pick us up in his big American car, a green Ford Galaxy. He took us to their house and to our surprise it was just like the image in the immigration film in Berlin. Their house was beautiful, with a rec room and a remarkably beautiful garden. Ria and Reinhardt looked after us as if they had known us a lifetime. To our surprise they were waiting for us; someone in Germany had told them that a young family would arrive from Darmstadt by ship to Canada, and then to Winnipeg. They helped us find a hotel for our first two nights, September 24 and 25, at the Madison Apartment Hotel, 210 Evanson Street. We paid ten dollars for two nights. They also helped us to find an apartment on Beverley Street almost right away. Ria was so kind and helpful. She came to set up the small apartment and surprised us with a home-baked cake and flowers, and she put on the kitchen table a table cloth and a lovely note in English, "Welcome to Canada." I am not sure any more but I probably had a little cry. Those are moments in life you do not forget. And Ria and Reinhardt became my wonderful friends for life.

On September 27, 1967, Sonja, who was six, started grade one at Greenway School. It was at first for her very difficult because she only spoke German. Then we moved to Edison Avenue, into a better apartment and she attended Springfield school. From here on Sonja and Volker attended many schools, sad to say, because we moved so much. When we immigrated here there was no language training provided for us. We had to learn English on our own. Johann could speak a little English. I do not remember ever a Canadian Government official asking how we were doing after we received the stamp into our passport in Quebec City. From there on we were on our own. The only people I ever remember visiting us on Edison Avenue were the ladies from the Welcome Wagon, local women who would go around and greet newcomers to their neighbourhoods. They gave me many advertising coupons and free samples. I used the free samples but I had no idea what the coupons were for.

Johann started at Lange's Konditorei on Ellice Avenue,

Sonja, Roswitha and Volker
First visit to Grand Beach Spring 1968

near Sherbrook Street, and I got my first part-time job after four months in Winnipeg. I shed many tears onto the floor of the Medical Arts Building where all I could get was a job as a cleaning lady. That is how I started life as an immigrant woman in the country of my dreams. It was a far cry from my days in Germany where I worked as a medical masseuse at the biggest hospital in Berlin. I guess most immigrants have to start at the bottom. But it seems a big waste of people's skills and training. And like most immigrants, I was also very homesick. But quickly I learned to speak some English, and that made it a little easier. However, that was just the beginning of the hard times that lay ahead.

Our first car 1968
A black Ford Galaxy 500

In the eight months we lived in Winnipeg I learned how to drive a car. The man who taught me to drive was German and when he found out that I had worked in a hospital and that I was a masseur, he said if I would give massages to his wife he would teach me how to drive. Great! That is what I did. I passed the driver's test the first time and received my driver's license in 1968. I have a lot to be grateful for to that

83

Sudbury 1968
Johann, Sonja and Volker
On our way to Montreal

German. He taught me well.

That first winter in Winnipeg was so hard we decided to move on to Montréal to a more cosmopolitan city and a less severe climate. Montréal would give us the music and the culture that we had left behind in Berlin. So we moved our few belongings and the children in our first car, a black Ford Galaxy 500 that we had bought for the one hundred dollars we had deposited in the Bank of Canada before leaving Germany.

It was a hard trip. The car needed oil every four to six hours or the engine would smoke, so we stopped many times on the roadside to fill up the oil. When we got to Sudbury we went to the police station and asked if we could park our car in their parking lot so we could sleep in the car. They said o.k. Once in a while an officer with a flashlight would check on us, and the next day they gave us coffee and doughnuts before we left. I think today that might not happen. The next morning we visited the nickel mine in Sudbury. The children were fascinated. Then we moved on and arrived in a small town in Ontario -- the name I do not remember. There we stayed in a cheap motel. We drove through Ottawa and went to see the Parliament Buildings and the Centennial Flame, then on to Montréal. We were so astounded by the beauty that this country had shown us, and here it began that I fell in love with Canada. But driving through Montréal was scary. I could not yet understand English very well, and on top of that I had to read all the French signs. But I had to do all the driving because, did I mention? Johann never learned to drive a car the whole time he was in Canada.

We found an apartment in Côte St-Luc, a suburb of Montréal and life began anew. Sonja and Volker went to school. We spoke only German at home but the kids continued to improve their English at school, and soon the two had made friends and were settled in. Johann first found a job in a bakery but music was always on his mind, and soon after he got a job playing at a jazz club on Rue Ste-Catherine. He was happy, but things were not so easy for the family. Yes, music is beautiful, but if one is involved with a band, most of the time he's performing at night and that life is not as glamorous as it seems. The audience enjoys the music as they listen, and the musicians love to play. But family life was hard because we didn't see Johann very much. He played at nights and in the day he needed to sleep and then practice his tenor saxophone and write music scores. He had to practice in the closet so the neighbors wouldn't hear him. I often resented that he spent so many hours on his music. Often some musician would come to our home and there was conversation about music, but I felt that he neglected the family. Yes, he brought music and intellectuality into our home, but it didn't feed the family and that was hard. Johann played at nights for eight months, and the club was always full with people. I had to drive at four a.m. to pick up Johann at the club. Then I had to get the kids up, give them breakfast and get them ready for school and be at work by nine a.m.

I was fortunate to find work in my profession as a masseur at an esthetics clinic run by Dr. Léonard on boulevard St-Joseph. What a great job it was! The clinic was of utmost elegance. Dr Léonard did various cosmetic procedures like breast lifting, eye lid correction, underwater massage and paraffin treatment. He hired me because when he showed me the *Siemens* medical instruments I was able to tell him that I had learned to use all those same instruments in Berlin.

But Montréal was not what Johann expected. The contract with the big band was finished and Johann found himself again in a bakery as a pastry chef. We still did not speak very good French, and that was a problem. So in 1969 we decided to move back to Winnipeg. He had found out that the music scene in Winnipeg was pretty lively and he hoped to find work. Also we had good friends there who wanted us back and they were very helpful in reestablishing us. But I regretted leaving Montréal and my job with Dr. Léonard. I was very well liked at the clinic and Dr. Léonard didn't want me to leave, and I did not know if I could find such a good job again in Winnipeg.

We sold the car in Montréal and travelled back by train to Winnipeg, By this time it was autumn, and we moved into the Cornwall Apartments on River Avenue. Johann got a job at the Hudson's Bay Company as a pastry chef. The store was very close to our apartment. He could walk over the Osborne Bridge and down Osborne past the Legislative Buildings to work. Our children had to start again at a new school, and I went to work part-time at the Vic Tanny Health Spa as a masseur. There I found out that masseur was not a respectable profession here in Winnipeg and it upset me, because I loved the job at Dr. Léonard's so much. At Vic

Tanny's I was almost ashamed to give massages to men and women because people did not understand the profession. Some people thought of it as a menial job, and others thought it was prostitution! Coming from a clinic like Dr. Léonard's I was very disappointed and I decided never ever to return to what I had learned in the health field in Germany. I did not want to degrade myself by a profession that I was so proud of. Today, of course, all that has changed, and there are very many therapeutic massage clinics in Winnipeg.

A short while later I found another job, as a waitress at the Pancake House on Pembina Highway. Mr. Gruberman, the owner, recognized how cheerful I was and how fast I learned to please the customers even though my English was still not very good. So he gave me chances to develop my English and at the same time he was very kind to me. There I learned about customer service and began to see how interesting the hospitality industry could be. I worked there for a year and a half. Winnipeg also gave Johann some satisfaction as he had the opportunity to play in the Ron Paley Big Band, and with some other musicians, but he continued to work at the Hudson's Bay Company.

I was able to save up money, and in June of 1970 I took Sonja and Volker for three weeks to Germany. I was so homesick and also wanted to reconnect with my father who had never met my children. Having lost my mother so young, my heart ached to find the other half of myself, and I wanted to know more about my father and where I came from. I had only met him twice, when he came to the cookie factory when I was sixteen, and then when he met with me and Monika, so I was very eager to spend more time with him. I had corresponded with him from Canada to an old address that I had found, so I could tell him I was coming.

As we arrived by train in Nürnberg, my father Heinrich was waiting to meet us on the platform. The reunion was warm and he had some chocolates for the children but he was not what I had expected. He was a man of about fifty-six years old and looking older. It seems that alcohol had taken its toll on him. He was almost blind and wore very thick glasses; it looked like cataracts or glaucoma.

We spent three days with him in his small apartment and talked for many hours about his life and the short marriage he had with my mom. He told me that he had loved my mom and that his love name for her was "Tilli". That was very important to me. He told me that before the War he had learned the trade of porcelain painter and worked for the Rosenthal company. This company was established in 1879, and is still famous for the quality of its products. I found out also that he had worked in Mannheim as a sign maker. He also was very athletic, and enjoyed gymnastics. I have some pictures of him doing acrobatics.

On this visit, my father introduced me to his sister, my Aunt Maria. Having another door opened on my past made me very happy. My aunt told me a little more about my father's life, that their mother went with him to the train as he left for the War. I have pictures of his mother saying goodbye to him, and a cross that was given to him by the Catholic nuns for a safe return. The cross was later given to me. Also I was told by my aunt that my father had another daughter in Germany, but where I do not know. I wondered why it had taken him so long to find us after the War – he came to the cookie factory some time in 1956 or 1957 – but he never said. I can only assume he had been looking for us in Cologne, and we were not there anymore.

My children most of the time had to play in their grandfather's bedroom while we talked. But he took us around to his favorite bars where he showed us off to his friends because he was so proud of us. And he wanted a souvenir of our visit, so he asked me to leave a Canadian dollar bill behind for the bar he loved, so he could remember us when we were gone, when he drank beer with his buddies.

Then he could tell his friends that his daughter and two grandchildren had come all the way from Canada to visit him.

Like Johann, my father was a musician. When he was a young man he wrote many music scores and musical plays that he performed with the band he had started during the War, named "Beno", when he played for Red Cross concerts and at the Officers' Mess. He also played in musicals and wrote music. After the War he still played, and I brought some of the posters advertising his performances back to Canada. I also have some scores that he wrote, but I do not know if his music has been performed since he retired from the band. Then it was time to go home to Canada. As my father and I said our farewells, I think we knew that we would not see each other again. On June 19, 1977, he died in Nürnberg. Sonja was in Germany at that time visiting her grandmother, so she attended his funeral and she brought some of his belongings back to Canada.

I have stayed in contact with my Aunt Maria, though. She is still alive and is now ninety-two years old and I have visited her a couple of times in Germany. Not long ago she sent me a beautiful tea set that had been made by the Rosenthal company, where my father had worked. On my last visit to her in 2000, she wanted to know more about me, so I told her stories about my past that she had not heard. That included my story about the doll my mother made for me and how I had wished for a real doll. To my surprise, at Christmas 2000, I received a parcel from Germany. I opened the parcel on Christmas Eve and my wish from childhood appeared. Out of a box came a beautiful doll, about twenty inches high, with long blond hair. She can open and close her blue eyes, she has soft rosy cheeks, and a little mouth like a heart. She is wearing a beautiful dress and has white socks and little shoes. In the box was also a note saying "Hi, I am Collette and I am yours." I was thrilled by my aunt's gift, and she was thrilled when I phoned her to tell her what a wonderful gift she gave me. Now my granddaughter Aria is in love with Colette and every time she comes over that is what she plays with. Many times she asks me, "Oma, can I take Collette home for a sleep-over?" and so she does.

On that same visit in 2000, to my surprise Aunt Maria introduced me to my father's older brother, Johann, an uncle I did not even know I had. It was a happy meeting but also very upsetting: how come I never knew that my father had a brother? My Aunt Maria and Uncle Hans, as I called him, took me to my father's grave and there I received my answer. My grandmother and grandfather had their names on the tombstone, but my father's name was nowhere to be found; Hans and Maria both told me that my father lies on the right-hand side of the grave where there was a little tree. I dearly wanted to ask why my father was buried apart from his family, but the look on my Uncle Han's face made me think that he and my father had a falling-out and then never spoke to each other again. I never found out what they quarreled about. I think it must have something to do with the war because I remember my father telling me that he hated the army but my uncle told me that he, for his part, had been a proud officer in the German army.

Again I was left alone with sadness to realize that I knew such a little bit about my father and my grandparents. Aunt Maria has only one daughter and I do not know much about her. Uncle Johann had never any children. It would have been good if I had known more family besides my mother and stepfather to help guide me as I was growing up.

I returned to Winnipeg with my two children and a year later I had my third child, a beautiful little girl we called Ilona. She was born on May 18, 1971 at the Women's Pavilion in what was then Winnipeg General Hospital and is now the Health Sciences Centre. I assure you, she did not make it easy for me. I had to go by city bus to the hospital three times with my little suitcase before she finally decided to come into the world. We were still living on River Avenue, and there we made wonderful friends with Sharon and Larry who also lived on River. Sharon was quite an artistic person. She did beautiful water-colour paintings and needlepoint and today her art work is well recognized. You can see her work at the Inn at the Forks in Winnipeg. We worked together at the Pancake House, and she helped me with my English. When Ilona was a baby, Sharon was a great help to me. Over the years we have shared many stories and laughs together.

Then in the fall of 1971 we moved again. Johann received an offer from Eaton's in Vancouver. A new Eaton's store was to open and they wanted him as their pastry chef because he had baked for Queen Elizabeth when she visited Winnipeg in 1970. Life started to look good with a new job and better pay, so off we went by train to Vancouver. There we first stayed in a hotel next to the train station till we found a nice town house in Burnaby. We settled into our new home and the kids really liked their school. Volker was in the third and Sonja in the sixth grade. Ilona had to go to a daycare because it was essential that I also work. So I found a job

Ilona one year old 1972

Ilona playing Princess 1973

91

at a Fairweather clothing store. There I worked part-time and found it was fun to sell those neat clothes. My English also started to improve.

I learned fast that I had to sell a lot to get a good commission. There was a board in the staff room and it showed each person's level of sales, so I knew what I had to achieve. Boy, did I learn fast! And I brought more money home so that we could have a better life. I dreamed of my own house and garden. I dreamed that my children would have a good future and a great education. Oh, I really started feeling on top of the world in Vancouver. For the first time in my life, things seemed to be going smoothly. Johann seemed happier too, and was easier to live with. He found places to play his music, but it did not take over our life.

In June, 1973 Johann read in a newspaper an advertisement about a bakery for sale in Fort Nelson, in northern British Columbia. He wanted to go there and to see it, find out what it was all about, but he became sick and he asked me to go instead. He looked after the children and I went. It sounded exciting that he wanted his own business. I flew to Fort Nelson and arrived at the small airport, then took a taxi

Joe's Bake Shop
Fort Nelson BC,1973

Manager.

For rent $200 mo. or sell, fully
equipped bakery, Fort Nelson, B.C.
Reply Box 3556, Province.

Commercial Real Estate Sales
Halworth Hold'nas Ltd. 324-2451

Advertising the Bake Shop

to the Fort Nelson Hotel where I met with the owner of the
bakery. We talked for a while and then an agent showed me
the Gateway Bakery, a small building with all the necessary
equipment. I took pictures of the entire inside and outside
for Johann to see. Some of the equipment was faulty and the
bakery hadn't been used for a long time. It smelled bad from
left-over sourdough.

But to me the bakery looked like a castle. In three days
I had all the papers ready from the fire, health and building
inspectors, and I found a small house for us to live in if we
decided to come. I went home to Vancouver very excited.
But it was still sad for us to leave Vancouver in July, 1973,
because we had settled in very nicely. For a while I was
not sure anymore if I made the right decision to tell Johann
about the bakery, but he said he very much wanted to quit
Eaton's because he was not happy there. And so it was we
moved again! We bought a Ford Bronco and packed our
belongings in. What couldn't fit in the car we tied onto the
roof. The three children sat in the back, and I drove us to
Fort Nelson. Being the driver was somehow exciting and
at the same time a big responsibility. And I worried that we
were now taking our children again to a different school and
to new friends. By this time, Ilona was a year and a half old,
Volker was nine, and Sonja was eleven.

The drive from Vancouver to Fort Nelson took two days.
We were full of enthusiasm and anticipation that now, finally,

Aug 10/1973

SCHARF FAMILY — Ilona, Joe, Volker, Sonja and Roswitha

Bakery To Open

A much needed long awaited business is to open up in Fort Nelson — A Bakery.

Joe and Roswitha Scharf with their three children, Sonja 13, Boker 10, Ilona 2 have come to take up residence here and to open the bake shop that will be known as Joe's Bakeshop.

Joe has experience with his European training, baked for Morgan's Store in Montreal, also the Hudson Bay Company in Winnipeg, Master Baker in Eaton's Vancouver and now to Fort Nelson to make his permanent home here with his family.

Mr Scharf has the distinction of being a Queen's Baker, for he was the Royal baker for Her Majesty when she visited Manitoba Centennial in 1970.

Pastries and such goodies are his specialties and apparently we can look forward to a large Fresh assortment of daily baked products.

Joe's Bakery will cater to the walk in trade and the people of Fort Nelson as well as the commercial and wholesale trade.

The inside of the bakery is being entirely refurbished, a new tile floor, washing, sealing, coating and paint job. The equipment is being all remodelled and replaced where necessary.

The Scharf's who are pristine in their outlook will not go into production until the place has been entirely cleaned and re-decorated and all in order but target date for the opening is around September 1, but watch for a sooner date.

Mrs Scharf will look after the counter and business end of the project and Joe will concentrate on his baking and pastry efforts. No hours or times are available at this time but they assure the News that they will adjust those to the customers' wishes.

"Bakery To Open"
August 10th 1973

94

we would find what we had been searching for. The drive from Vancouver to Fort Nelson was like a little holiday. We stopped at every beautiful sight on the Alaska Highway and showed our children the beauty of this country. The first day we drove all the way to Fort St. John, where we stayed overnight. The next day we travelled the last six hundred miles to Fort Nelson. We received such a warm welcome from the people of Fort Nelson! It was so overwhelming we could hardly believe it. There were newspaper items about us, and people couldn't wait for the day that we opened the bakery with fresh breads, buns and pastries. We moved into the little pink house that I had found, and we made it comfortable and cozy. Then we went to work for one month to bring the bakery up to health and safety standards. Sonja and Volker helped with the cleaning and scraping while, for Ilona, we found a very nice English woman named Anne Boyer who had two children of her own and also baby-sat other children. She gave a lot of love to my Ilona and took very good care of her.

The day we opened Joe's bake shop it was unbelievable! People lined up at eight a.m. to be the first in the bakery to buy our fresh goods. By two in the afternoon we were sold out of everything and we had to close the bakery to start all over again. This became our routine. Johann and I started very early. Then I needed to go home to get the children ready for school and then I went back to the bakery by nine. The days were very long, but the bakery was very successful.

The children adapted very well to their new home. They made friends and some of their friends wanted to help in the bakery. Often we even had Ilona working. We would sit her on the dough table and she learned at three years old how to roll buns. Volker learned how to bake and cut the bread in the bread machine and Sonja and I became the salesgirls. We were the talk of the town. People came from everywhere for bread and Johann's wonderful pastry and our friendly service. We had been city people and now were living in a small town of 2500 people. It was a big adjustment for Johann and me, but the children loved it. I remember Volker telling me how much he liked living there and hoped we would stay there. Besides making friends, he played hockey, and Sonja learned to ice skate in the arena.

Fort Nelson was a great town with a hospital, schools, and one main street. It has its own airport, and in those days its own newspaper. Joe's bake shop was right on the Alaska Highway. Everybody knew everybody else. There was only one motel in town, also right on the Highway. Many tourists came by to buy our breads and pastries and we met people from all over the world. They came with their silver Airstreams and other motor homes. The town is surrounded

"Joe's bake shop"
Volker and Sonja 1973

Bake Shop Opens

JOE ANXIOUSLY waiting at the oven to put the finishing touches on his goods.

ROSWITHA arranging a try of tempting treats.

To say the Bakeshop had a successful opening is hardly an adequate discription. The public's response to this opening was unbelievable. People started lining up at 8:30 waiting for the doors to open at 9. The customers were so anxious to buy fresh bakery goodies most of them didn't take time for coffee and treats. By noon it was necessary to have a short two hour closure to replenish the depleted bakery supply. At opening time the display cases and shelves were full to over flowing plus the cooling racks in the baking area were brim full, but with such a great response the shelves were soon bare, a true indication of the need for a Bakery.

We extend best wishes to Joe and Roswitha and their family on their new business venture.

Wedding belles are ringed during the ceremony—and let's not bother about the grammar of that statement.

"Bake Shop Open" 1973

by a great forest. The town lies on a slope. If you drove all the way to the top by the hospital you could see very far. In the evenings I was always amazed when there were northern lights, which were astounding, and much brighter than the ones we see sometimes here. I have never forgotten them to this day; they still fascinate me. On one winter Sunday we watched sled-dog races and a street parade where the whole town participated. It was wonderful to see the whole community come together like that.

I wanted to stay too, and I hoped that we would put down roots here. But once again Johann was not happy. The town was so small there was not much interest in music, and we only had a small radio in the bakery for Johann to listen to. To be fair to him, it was also a hard life for him. The bakery took many long hours to run, and he was all the time over-tired. My hope to succeed in Fort Nelson began to diminish. After seven years criss-crossing Canada, our spirit of adventure was low, and we could not decide where was best to settle down, in Canada or in Germany. It is an immigrant's dilemma. Some of my friends who came earlier to Canada had the same problem. It is not possible not to be homesick and compare our homelands with Canada. The old country has culture and history for hundreds and hundreds of years, and Canada only started to be settled by Europeans about five hundred years ago. There was not even a city of Winnipeg until after 1850! This is what drives the European immigrants back home; they will sell everything they own and use their last pennies to return, only to find out that they have changed, and then have to return to Canada only to start all over again. Some never can go home because of the financial burden.

Finally we decided to sell out and return to Germany. The *IGA* in Fort Nelson bought our bakery and with that money and our savings we returned to Germany. These were very unsettling times for our children as we packed up our belongings and we drove back over the Yellow Head Highway with our Ford Bronco to Winnipeg. We left our car in Winnipeg with our friends Karl and Doris, and took the train to Montréal to return to Germany on the last boat to leave in December of 1974.

So here we were back in Montréal boarding the same ship, the *S.S. Maasdam*, except the ship had been sold to the Polish Ocean Lines, and was renamed the *Stephen Batory*. We went through the same routines as before, and nothing had changed in the interior of that ship, only the bar was now a disco bar with nightly dancing.

We stayed six months in Germany till May, 1975. Johann worked as a pastry chef and played music on the side with his brother, who is also quite a famous jazz musician in Germany. Lothar Scharf is much known. He had a drum school in Darmstadt and has travelled with his band all over Europe and Africa. He studied in Berlin, first classical music and then jazz.

While we were there, for the first time I did not go to work but stayed home with the children to help them adjust to German life. But it was not long before we realized that we had changed and didn't feel at home in Germany any more. We had integrated into the Canadian ways of life and our home sickness was now for Canada. We missed the big blue sky and the freedom that we had discovered in our travelling across Canada and the friendly people in it. So what to do? Return to Canada again! Johann returned first alone to Vancouver in April of 1975 only to find out that there was no work for him. I came a month later to Vancouver with Ilona, who was now four, and with what was left of our savings. Sonja and Volker stayed in Germany with their grandmother.

7

BREAKING UP, BREAKING DOWN

Ilona became very sick on the flight back to Canada, and our arrival in Toronto was not very pleasant. A doctor had to come onto the airplane and all the passengers had to wait until he gave the o.k. that everyone could get off the plane. Some passengers complained. I went on to Vancouver and we took Ilona to a hospital where we discovered that she needed a small bladder operation. After all the disappointment in Germany and the worries of moving back to Canada and Ilona being sick, I was devastated to learn that Johann had a new lover. He had met her in Montréal, and even though she was a stranger to him, he took her with him to Vancouver where they stayed with a friend of ours. I was extremely hurt and angry, and my feelings for him began to change. Then, with no work and a small sick child, we returned to Winnipeg by train in May, 1975.

Our family problems were serious and our marriage was in trouble. I had gone wherever Johann wanted to, and done what I hoped would make him happy, but all the moving, the effects on the children's happiness, and his unfaithfulness were becoming too much for me. I was now thirty-five years old and we had achieved very little, only stress on the children, heartache and disappointment for me, and no lasting success.

We stayed in Winnipeg at Motel 75 on Pembina Highway for three months in a room that had a small kitchen, and then moved to an apartment on Pembina. In the meantime, Volker and Sonja returned from Germany. They were now twelve and fourteen years old and started school in Fort Garry. I feel so bad for them when I look back at our life, never giving them a chance, except in Fort Nelson, to really feel at home, and then taking them away from there.

At least our friends Karl and Doris had looked after our car, so we had a car again. Johann found work again as a pastry chef at the Dominion food store at Polo Park, and I gathered up my courage to look for a new job. All the time we were in Canada I tried to improve my English by reading newspapers and watching TV. I found out there was a new trendy restaurant about to open on Osborne Street called Basil's. The owner was looking for a manager. So, with no experience as a manager, but a lot of determination inspired by the need for a job, I applied and I was hired on August 15, 1975 as the first manager. I had a staff of twenty-six people. Basil, the owner, became my mentor in how to run a restaurant; he gave me also the chance to pioneer the first *avant-garde* restaurant in Osborne Village. I worked extremely hard for long hours and my sense of achievement and my confidence began to grow. But very often I felt pain, knowing that I had to neglect my family to make money so we could survive.

I was manager of Basil's Restaurant for seven years. We bought our first small house at 177 Wardlaw Avenue with a little down-payment to the bank. I began to be a little hopeful again as Johann seemed a bit happier. But then he was hired at CKJS 810 to work as a disk jockey at night, so he quit his job at Dominion. He worked at the radio station for two years, but his income was not enough for a family of five. Our marriage did not improve, and I became more and more unhappy. Then in 1977 I met a gentleman I'll call Roland who would change my whole life.

Roland was a very handsome man of Asian background. He had a deep and mysterious aura, and he told me he was a martial arts expert with many black belts. He came often to Basil's and we became friends. I started to pour my heart out to him. I told him about my personal life from childhood to marriage. More and more I talked with him, and all my emotions got stirred up. I do not know how it happened, but he would come into the restaurant and my heart would start thumping and my stomach would feel funny and before I knew it I was completely infatuated with him. He gave me a ring that had belonged to his mother. I thought he gave it to me for spiritual strength to survive the difficult times, but I don't really know what he meant by it because no words had been exchanged. The ring that he gave me was of old gold with a ruby stone. He handed it to me at the restaurant. In one of our conversations something happened; I experienced a deep warm love in my spirit that I had never experienced before. But after a while we did not talk so much. My work had to continue at the restaurant, even though I was drawn to him. When he came to visit the restaurant only our eyes spoke to each other. How desperately I wanted to talk to him! Now I was overworked, unhappy with Johann, and emotionally drained and I did not understand what was happening to me. In the restaurant everyone noticed my behavior. I thought I needed to talk to Johann and ask him to help me. It was Christmas of 1977; it was the worst Christmas we ever had.

I told Johann about Roland and my feelings for him. I thought he would try to understand like I did when he was unhappy. I forgave him for his lovers, but he could not forgive my infatuation with Roland. I realized that Johann could not do this, because he was more like my fourth child than my husband and spiritually not aware of my pain.

Early in the New Year we got a legal separation and Johann found himself an apartment. What confusion! What drama! Twenty-two years we were together and now it was all crumbled. Then after Johann moved out, I lost the house to the bank because I could not make the payments and feed and clothe the children, so the four of us moved to Nassau Avenue into an apartment in a house. I still managed Basil's restaurant and I worked hard to stay on top of everything. But by the fall of 1978 I was nearly breaking down again. I hadn't seen Roland for a long time, but my longing to talk to him and my deep feelings for him were unbearable. Then I saw him coming into the restaurant with another woman. He ignored me completely. I felt my heart was broken.

I collapsed in the restaurant office holding the ring that Roland had given me, and ended up in Victoria Hospital for three months with physical, emotional and mental exhaustion. My nervous system was shot and I could not stop crying. All the time, I only could think about my children and ask myself what had happened to me. Johann came only once to visit me. He gave me a box of chocolates and said he didn't understand how anyone could do that to herself. My children visited me very often and my son came even by bicycle to see me. I decided that I must get out of the hospital and asked the nurse if I could go to the park for walks.

I started to take a brisk walk every day and when I felt stronger sometimes I ran for an hour at a time. Soon I was feeling much better. I strongly felt that my mother's spirit was present with me, and I talked to her in my mind. I also had a good friend named Klaus who came every day on his lunch hour to visit me, and I could lean on his shoulder and cry as he comforted me.

I only saw Roland a few more times after that. The first time was after I had left Basil's. Our conversation was very short because my heart still ached. Later, when I had my own restaurant, The Tea Cozy, he came visiting and brought me a red rose. Then I was able to have a normal conversation with him. It seemed that my feelings for him had healed, and I have never seen him again. But I know now he was the bridge to my new life. The pain I experienced is not possible to describe, but healing from it made me much stronger than

I was before.

Veronica and Henry were the owners of the house where I rented our apartment. They were very good friends to me. Veronica helped me through my hard times and she looked after my Ilona. Her kindness I will never forget. She was like an angel sent from heaven. The two older children had to look after themselves in our rented apartment all the time I was at work, but they were good, responsible children. I was very proud of them.

At Christmas, 1978, Johann moved back into our apartment and some little hope grew that we would have our family together again. In January of 1979 he decided to go to Toronto for a new job and then send for the family later. At least that is what he said he was going to do. But it never happened. He met another woman and he returned with her to Germany.

Over and over I asked myself "What have I done?" My shame towards my children was very deep. I thought it was my fault that my marriage had fallen apart and their father left. I became very disillusioned and hopeless. I continued to work very hard at Basil's. I had no choice because I was now the only income earner for the four of us. It was difficult to manage on one income, so in the middle of May I decided to phone Dr. Léonard in Montréal and see if my old job in his clinic would be available for me, because I would earn more there. He was pleased to hear from me and told me I could start any time. I resigned from *Basil's* and with the little courage I had left and the little money I had saved, we packed our belongings and moved again to Montréal, hoping once more to get a start.

We flew to Montréal and found an apartment on rue Sherbrooke. We lived extremely poor in Montréal and emotionally I was not healthy yet. I tried to phone Johann in Germany to help us, but no response. Life seemed so sad. Luck was not on my side. Now there were only three of us, me, Volker and Ilona, because Sonja had decided in May, before we left Winnipeg, to go to Germany and visit her grandmother and to be with her father.

Having very little money in Montréal, I decided to go to a government office for help. I explained to a man who worked there my situation and told him that I had a job offer but I was right now very short of money. I only needed a little help. He gave me a lot of papers to fill out but as I read through them I felt insulted. I told the man I did not need his charity and I walked out of his office. I then found out to my terrible disappointment that the job at Dr. Léonard's was no longer available for me, because the woman who was supposed to leave had changed her mind. What to do? I took a job in a hamburger and deli restaurant on Rue Sherbrooke for five months. My inner strength was being tested again, and I did not feel very strong. I cried a lot and I began to pray. And my prayer was answered! In the beginning of November, 1979, after living four months in Montréal I received a call from Winnipeg. My old boss Basil asked me to return to Winnipeg and manage his restaurant again. It was a blessing and I agreed to come back right away. Basil was very kind and paid the return trip to Winnipeg for the three of us, and he also helped us find a home on River Avenue. His kindness touched in my heart and I will never forget all that he did for me.

Sonja returned to Winnipeg from Germany in June of 1980 to be with her family here in Winnipeg again, and I worked for the next three years for Basil. But the restaurant reminded me always of Roland and what had happened to me and Johann. I could no longer continue working in the restaurant. I let both men cause me so much pain, and sometimes I wondered what spirit guided me through all of it so I could finally break away from the past and begin all over. I hoped if I could become my own whole person maybe happiness would come to me.

8

ARRIVAL

My life became a carousel. Johann left us with no financial support, and I was devastated that he had abandoned the children like that. When our divorce was automatically made final in March, 1982, after three years' separation, Johann was not even living in Canada and I was on my own. Here began the most difficult test of my life. I needed to use all my will power and cling to my faith if I wanted to survive emotionally and physically, so I went on praying.

In January 1982 I was sent for a bladder operation and on my return to work in February I knew I could not keep working at Basil's because I was no longer as strong as I was before the operation. Also, Basil needed a manager who could run his restaurant without all the emotional history that was tangled up in his business for me. The memories of what had happened in my life while I managed the restaurant would come back every time I went to work.

I was immediately hired to be the manager of Swallows restaurant, another trendy place that had opened a few years before at the corner of Osborne and River Avenue. It was a Danish-style restaurant upstairs in a renovated building where downstairs Victor's restaurant was. I worked there for seven months. With my small savings from an income tax refund, I went back to Germany with my youngest child, Ilona, in an attempt to decide if I should return permanently to my homeland. I also sold my car because I needed more money for the trip. My Canadian friend of many years,

Judith, had warned me that it would not be easy for me to go to Germany because I had set down roots here. She was right, and I am very grateful to have such a good, loyal friend. She often gives me comfort and wise advice. I also quickly found out that Sonja and Volker, now young adults, would never come with me to Germany and I was not able to leave them behind. They were Canadians! They were both working in restaurants and they had their own friends and their own lives. They were both mature; all our moving around and resettling in different places and starting all the time new schools made them strong and adaptable. As well, their father leaving them and my break-down made them grow up fast. When I realized how strong were the roots my children had put down in Canada, I realized that Germany was in my past and my future was in Canada by their side.

My many years working in restaurants gave me a good knowledge of the hospitality industry, and I knew that I must venture to run my very own business and be my own boss. My brother Horst and I had got together on my visit in Germany and we discussed our lives, where we were and where we were going. He was just going through a divorce and he was also disillusioned with his life. He decided to help me.

I got back to Winnipeg in May of 1982 and I went back to working at Swallows. Volker had left school and was living on his own and working at Moskowitz & Moskovitz, a restaurant on Main Street, near the bridge. One day he invited me to meet him there, and sat me down at a table in front of a window. There was a little car parked outside, and he asked me, "What do you think of that car?" I asked him if he had bought it, and said how pleased I was that he had earned enough money for it. "You deserve it," I said. He looked at me and said, "Mom. That car is for you!" I was so surprised and touched I do not know what I said to him. Maybe I was speechless! But I will never forget how he told me the car was for me, and I remember we both went for a car-ride right away. It made me so happy to think what thoughtfulness and love came from my son. I named the car "Lulu" for good luck, and I think it was lucky for me. Not long after, a good friend, Don, who was the owner of the Dutchmaid Ice Cream store in Osborne Village, advised me that The Tea Cozy Restaurant, just a few doors down Osborne from Basil's towards River, was for sale; the woman who owned it wanted after four years of running it to retire.

The Tea Cozy Restaurant
Osborne Village, Winnipeg, Manitoba

As I entered The Tea Cozy to inquire about the sale of the restaurant, I felt I was lifted up into a new world. I sat at a small table and looked around the room and I could see my future. I felt full of energy and anticipation, and I just knew that this was the right direction to go. The owner knew that I had restaurant experience and that I would be a good owner of her place, and she waited until I received the money from

Horst to sell the restaurant to me. Within a short time, and with the financial help from Horst, I acquired The Tea Cozy on October 15, 1982. I was so excited that I could use all I had learned about the restaurant business and apply it here in my very own place. I felt strong and energetic, and full of hope for the future. I had not felt like that for a long time. The very next day I took possession of the restaurant, keeping the same employees. The next morning the former owner was supposed to help me get to know the customers and introduce me to my new employees. Instead, she came to the back door of the restaurant, handed me the keys and said: "You know what you are doing; here are the keys and from here on you're on your own!" I was surprised and a little bit frightened, but I knew I had no choice. I walked up into the restaurant and into the small office, took a deep breath, and walked out to meet the employees. I said: "we can start to work now". But I will save the rest of this story for the next chapter.

In the meantime, my personal and family life began to be much happier. I was able to go in September, 1984, on my first real holiday. I was now forty-four years old, and I had never gone on a trip that wasn't full of anxiety about finding work and finding a place to live and worrying about my family. What an exciting adventure for me! I went to Club Med in Mexico, to Playa Blanca for seven days. On my way there I made great friends with some French girls from Montréal and we stayed together at the resort and flew back to Canada together. When we first got to Club Med, we were greeted with champagne and got to check everything out. My room was in a large building put quite high on a hill. The building was made out of red and brown clay and tiles. My bed was on a platform also made out of red stone, and a bright blanket covered it. As I looked out of my window I could see the sea foaming with waves and hear the powerful roaring of the surf as it crashed onto the white sandy beach. I felt like I was in heaven. I took a deep breath of the wonderful ocean air, and then I got ready to enjoy every single moment of my seven days in paradise.

The time went by so quickly! There was dancing, the resort put on shows, I went swimming and I learned how to steer a sail boat. I was asked if I would like to compete in an arm-wrestling competition. I guess they could see what good strong arms I had from all my hard work. So I said yes. What fun it was! And I won! I received a Club Med tee shirt. The bar was a new experience for me. One gentleman must have noticed that I was shy and that I followed the girls always. He asked me to go swimming with him and I was perplexed. What kind of question was that? But anyway, I said o.k., not thinking much about it. After supper all the girls went with our bathing suits and shawls to the bar and I forgot all about the arrangement with the man. But he did not forget. He came into the bar and said, "Well, are you ready to go for that swim?" I looked at him and told him it was too dark out there on the beach. Everyone at the bar laughed and the girls encouraged me to go on. I said to the man, "Well, you need to change first into a swim suit." He dropped his pants so fast I was shocked – but he was wearing his swim suit underneath and said "I'm all ready!"

My friends told me they would look out for me so I decided to go with him. It seemed very dark on the beach at first, but the light from the bar shone towards the water and the moon was very high, so soon I could see o.k. There was a gentle breeze from the sea and the waves were washing up onto the beach. I sat myself on the fine white sand and let the gentle waves come over my body. I started crying and laughing at the same time. I had forgotten that the man was still with me until he laughed and told me that in his lifetime he had never seen someone so happy they were crying and laughing at the same time. It really was paradise for me.

Four years later, love came into my life when I met my

husband, Camille. This is how I met him. On March 5, 1988, I went for the first time to a dance at a singles' club with my friend, Roswitha, who was visiting from Germany. That evening there was a special on for new members, so I signed up and paid my first membership fee of forty-two dollars. I always said it was the best investment I ever made. That was the only time I ever attended a singles' club. We played games, threw darts and sipped our glasses of wine. But as the evening went on, I wanted to go home. I did not feel comfortable in a place where most of the people knew each other. But then the dancing started and I changed my mind. I love to dance, and I hadn't had a chance for a long time, so I decided after all to stay for a while.

It just so happened that Camille was sitting right in front of me at another table. I saw a gentleman with beautiful curly brown hair and he noticed me. As the music began he asked me to dance. We danced and talked and laughed through the evening until the end. When Camille asked me my name, both my friend Roswitha and I introduced ourselves to him. Poor Camille! He looked so confused; never had he meet two women with the same name on the same evening. How we laughed! I learned that he had been separated and was lonely like me. And we became a couple. In June of 1988 when I proudly became a Canadian citizen, after the swearing-in ceremony at the federal courtroom it was Camille who draped the Canadian flag around my shoulders and presented me with a little stuffed beaver bearing the Canadian flag and the words "Canadian, Eh!"

On March 5, 1989, Camille and I got engaged at the Royal Crown Restaurant, high above the city with the beautiful sparkling lights that looked like stars in the night sky. What a romantic evening! As we sat across from each other, one could feel that love was in the air. We exchanged gifts, and I discovered that Camille had hidden a fancy decorated little box in a beautiful bouquet of roses. Inside was a golden ring with a ruby in the middle, surrounded with eight diamonds that sparkled like the stars. It was a beautiful way to begin the joining of our two lives together. My children met Camille and they were very happy for me that I had met a wonderful, gentle man like him. They liked him and wanted to see me happy. So here began again a new chapter.

In May of 1989 we decided to move in together and so I arranged for Ilona to stay in a small apartment. She wanted so badly to live on her own like her brother and her sister. She was now eighteen years old and she assured me that she could do it. I hoped that she was mature enough, but I was mistaken. The freedom of living on her own was too much for her. She fell in love with a young man and then the two of them made me a grandmother. On July 7, 1990, Ilona, nineteen years old, gave birth to my first beautiful grandchild, Tanisha. What an experience! I stayed with her through the birth. To see my daughter bearing my grandchild, it was like a miracle. But I spent many hours in the hospital worrying if she could make it on her own. Many anxious thoughts went through my mind.

As the old saying goes, the apple falls not far from the tree. I thought, "Well, Ilona has strength and determination like her mother. I know my daughter. She will do the right thing for herself and her baby." And she did. She made me very proud. She went back to school and finished her grade twelve at Grant Park Collegiate, across Grant Avenue from her small apartment. My granddaughter became the first baby to attend Grant Park Collegiate in a program where young mothers could take their babies and look after them while they finished school. But it sure was not easy for her. She helped in The Tea Cozy as a server, went to school and looked after her baby. I helped in my motherly way and often my grandchild came to the restaurant, so she had a special place under one table all of her own. After graduation, Ilona continued her education as a hairstylist, still raising her little girl by herself.

Meantime, in 1988, my Sonja, who had also helped at The Tea Cozy and worked in other restaurants, had saved up enough money to quit her job and enroll at the Northern Alberta Institute of Technology in Edmonton, where she completed the two-year professional photography program. We flew to Edmonton to be at her side for her graduation in 1990 and gave her a big bouquet of flowers. How proud I was to see her achieve her goal. After graduating, she landed in Vancouver and spent the next five years assisting some of the top professional photographers in B.C. She started her own studio in 1995, shooting mainly for fashion and commercial clients. In 1998 she moved to Toronto. There she spends most of her time producing art photography. She worked on images for her solo shows at the Art Gallerie Gora in Montréal and the Edward Day Gallery in Toronto and many others. Her work is astonishing. Here is her own description of what her images say:

> *The human drive to find spirituality in life and in the common and cross-cultural belief in a Creator or a Divine Intelligence has influenced many artists. The spiritual needs and aspirations of the human spirit, represented by the higher self (the good) are in constant battle with the shadow side of the psyche, represented by the ego (the evil). Myths, symbols and personifications – divine or otherwise -- help us to understand the archetypes that are at play in all of these aspects of life.*

Someone said about her: "she is questioning and exploring the paradox of human experience as well as our struggle to find our own spiritual path and to surrender to the lessons we all must learn to reach our highest potential".

When Sonja was nineteen, she had come to me to tell me that she was gay. At first I did not know what to do with that.

I questioned myself many times: "Have I done something to trigger that behavior? Is there something wrong with her?" But then she gave me a book to read, *Different Daughters,* by Louise Rafkin. I realized being gay was just what some people are, and there was nothing wrong with it, and that I had not "made" her gay. I decided to learn more about her feelings and joined her with her friends at the club she always went to. There I realized that she was not the only one and my love for my daughter grew. I knew she had realized very young who she is and I fully respected that. Today she is forty-six years old and happy with her partner, and my love for her, as for my other children, is unconditional.

My son focused on his ultimate dream sport, the triathlon, where he achieved high standards and recognition. He was named in his sport as the fastest triathlete cyclist in Manitoba in 1989. He had also gone out on his own very young, but he succeeded in his sport. But he had disappointment too. His dream to go to the Olympics in 1992 did not become a reality because of the financial burden. He is also an artist. He does beautiful stone etchings. Some of his work can be seen at the Bikes and Beyond Shop in Winnipeg. He also found his niche in life with his wife, Natasha. Looking back on what my children have achieved and how successful as human beings they are, I must say I am so proud of them.

My grandchild, Ilona's daughter Tanisha, had during this time become the joy of my life and filled my heart with love for her. So when Ilona decided to move to Toronto to continue her education and became a specialist in curly hair texture, I thought my heart would break to lose Tanisha. In Toronto, Ilona met her future husband, Tracy, and once again I had to remember that I live in Canada and that in a multi-cultural nation like ours, we are not to judge whom our children fall in love with by where they come from. Tracy, who is Canadian, was born in Barbados and with his parents, like my elder children and me, came to Canada as immigrants. Camille and I flew to Toronto and, with my two other children at my side, we gave our blessings to Tracy and Ilona, and to Tanisha.

Ilona was a beautiful bride. On their wedding day, I read this poem to them:

TO ILONA.

In our wonderful homeland, an old custom there be,
To pass on to the children, the "fruit of our tree."
A gift of great meaning to start your new life,
When you've said your "I do's" and become a new wife.

On October the first, in the year "Y2K"
You'll stand before God, and your vows you will say.
Here's a German tradition I pass on to you,
And then to Tanisha you should pass it on, too.

The bread is to ward off hunger and strife,
And then there is salt, the essence of life.
The last is a coin, so you'll always have money,
May the rest of your days be happy and sunny.

And from Mother to Daughter, a little advice,
Love is the bounty of everyone's life.
Give of it freely, to those that you choose,
But Love should be cherished, and never abuses.

That poem was written by a dear friend who took my words and wove them together.

She also helped me write a poem for Tracy:

On your wedding day today I wish you the gift of time.
I hope that from this moment on your life will be sublime.
You take Ilona as your wife, Tanisha as your child:

May your life with both of those I love forever be beguiled.
Time is such a curious thing, it's never standing still,
Like the everlasting winds of change, orr the ink-flow from a quill.
Time is something you must take with those surrounding you.
Some times can hurt, some times can heal, some times can be so bright,
Like watching rainbows after storms, or the moon and stars at night.
Time is there to use at will, so use it carefully.
Time will mean so very much to your loving family.
So take this time I wish you to make a brand new start,
And take the love I wish you from the bottom of my heart.

Ilona and Tracy later had a new daughter. They called her Aria. My Ilona is a great mom and Tracy a wonderful dad. Not long after Aria was born, Ilona and her family moved from Toronto back to Winnipeg. As I write this, Aria is five years old, and to my joy I can teach my Princess my German language at the *Kinderschule.* Tanisha is now sixteen years old and a great basketball player at Churchill Collegiate, but she's still my "Dudele". And I am so proud of all three of my children, and grateful that I could love them and raise them to be good, hard-working people and proud Canadians.

Camille and I were happily married on September 21, 1990, on my fiftieth birthday, at the Shriners' Temple on Wellington Crescent, surrounded by our dearest friends and our families. I had a most beautiful dress made of white Italian lace with pearls, and I wore a daisy crown and carried a basket of daisies. And then there were the shoes!

In the old country, there is a custom that the bride-to-be must save her pennies to buy her wedding shoes. So I had saved pennies for two years, and when it was time to buy the shoes, I poured all the pennies out on the floor. Then my groom-to-be had to take a penny from the pile, and hold onto it until I danced with him at our wedding. Then he was to place the penny in my shoe for the first dance to bring us good luck and happiness. As it turned out, we did not dance on our wedding day because we had decided instead to have a cocktail reception after the ceremony. So I gave up on that part of the custom.

On the day of our wedding, I followed another old German custom. My maid of honour, Judy, had to help me out of my old clothes and into everything new. We sipped champagne as we did this. Then, at seven p.m., with our seventy-five guests waiting below, I walked down the grand staircase holding Volker's arm. We came down the stairs to the sound of guitar played by Dana Starkell,

My Wedding, September 21 1990
"My childhood make-believe!"

a piece by Robert De Visée called *Suite for a King*. As I walked slowly down the stairs I could see the love shining in Camille's eyes, and I knew I had achieved my dreams. I had come home.

We were married by Ian MacDonald, and made our vows in three languages: English, German and French. My maid of honour, Judy, read a poem in English, and Camille's brother, Justin from Québec, read the same poem in French, while our best man, Manfred Pump, read it in German. After that, everybody toasted us with champagne, and there was a lot of hugging and laughing and crying from happiness.

That New Year's Eve, Camille and I were invited to the Ball at Fort Garry Hotel Grand Ballroom. I wore my beautiful lace dress and white shoes, and Camille was dressed all in his best. I must say, we looked fantastic! Then, after we had all cheered in the New Year, Camille asked me to dance the first dance with him. As we stepped onto the dance floor,

September 21,2007. Married seventeen years.

he stopped me before I could begin the graceful dance in my beautiful shoes. He bent down and took from his jacket pocket the penny he had chosen all those months before and put in my left shoe. I was surprised and delighted and very happy that he had remembered the old custom. And it did bring us happiness and luck.

In 1991, with Camille's encouragement, I went back to school, at the age of fifty-one, to Adult Education to learn English grammar. One cannot imagine how hard it was to go two times a week to school after a full day's working in The Tea Cozy, and sit in a classroom with so many young students. A lot of them were younger than my own children. Sometimes students would ask me, "How come you are so long in Canada and only now you are attending school?" That was hurtful and embarrassing. On one occasion, my teacher allowed me to speak to the class. I explained that in my time of immigration, 1967, there were not the same services as there are now. I told them: "You are getting paid for going to school but in my time we had to learn the language on our own and go to work to make a living." After my speech, the teacher was impressed by my well-spoken English and he said to the others, "You all have a lot to learn from her, and do you know she still has to pay for her own schooling now?" After that every one was much nicer to me. And then they found out that I had a business. I had tried so hard to keep work separate from the school as I knew that they would come and ask me for jobs that I could not give them. It was very disappointing for them and sad for me that I could not hire any of them.

I took classes five long years, but my determination paid off and I finished Grade 12 English in 1996. Eager to learn more, I continued for two more years with computer courses.

Then, after I started teaching German at the *Kinderschule*, I decided to further my studies and started childcare courses at Red River College. Soon I had seven certificates in Early Childhood Education from the Manitoba Childcare Association. In January of 2007, I returned to Red River to complete another certificate part-time. This summer (2007) I have completed a forty-hour course at Red River which qualified me as an assistant teacher in kindergarten.

I am very happy with what I have chosen to do in the latter years of my life. The child-care job is a kind of completion on my childhood, because I had then little opportunity to play or freedom to explore the world. The courses and the teaching have opened up that whole world for me, and as I express myself naturally to the children, it is as if I am a child again, but with grown-up knowledge and experience and responsibilities.

9

THE TEA COZY

As my personal and family life flourished, my business became also very successful. After I purchased The Tea Cozy in 1982, it became my challenge to put into use everything I had learned in the hospitality industry. I was optimistic and disciplined, and I toiled sixty hours a week to make the restaurant a success. My three children all believed in me and they worked so hard with me I can't thank them enough, but finally we had a better and more peaceful life than ever before.

My brother Horst was to come to Canada on January 24, 1984. He arranged to buy a house on McLennan Road near Lockport. I moved there from River Avenue until he got to Canada to get his house settled as my good deed to him. But it became a chore for me. Ilona had to go to the Lockport School and I drove from there to Winnipeg and back every day for six months until Horst arrived as a landed immigrant.

My most memorable Christmas was 1983, just before Horst arrived. On Christmas Eve, I had closed my business, and put all the money from the week, which included the employees' pay cheques, in a bank bag. I gave it to one of the kids to carry home to Lockport in their backpack. However, as we left the restaurant and began loading the car, we became distracted by things we still had to do for Christmas, and also worried about driving to Lockport because a terrible snowstorm had just come upon us. Quickly we got into the car and began driving home, all the while forgetting that my bank bag in the backpack had been placed on top of the car as we rearranged our seating. By the time we reached home the snowstorm was very bad, and then we discovered the backpack was missing. We searched everywhere we could think of in the car and the house, but we couldn't drive back to the city to look for it there because the storm was too bad.

Despite our loss, we tried hard to celebrate Christmas Eve. Unfortunately our anxiety about the lost bag and its contents effectively spoiled our celebration of that special night. All seemed lost when, at 2:00 a.m. Christmas morning, Winnipeg police officers knocked at our door and presented us with the lost bag. We were thrilled as the police explained that a young couple, while walking over the Osborne Street Bridge, had spotted the money lying all over the road. These wonderful people had unselfishly gathered up all the money and put it back in the bag which they found nearby. Then, without identifying themselves, they brought the money and bag to the police. The money was all there, including credit cards and bill slips and the employees' pay cheques. I had received from Germany a couple days before a parcel for Christmas and in there was German Christmas *stollen* (the stollen is made with raisin and glazed orange and lemon peals; my favorite part is the marzipan. It is similar to an English fruit cake, but not as moist as a fruit cake.) I gave the *stollen* over to the two police officers to thank them for helping us, and shed a few tears of joy over the returned bag. The care and honesty of the young couple who found it was true Christmas spirit, and helped make that Christmas Day a truly special one.

Once Horst was settled in at Lockport, I moved back to Winnipeg to Hay Street, so I did not have the long drive back and forth to Lockport every day. My brother and I became co-owners of The Tea Cozy. Not too long after, his future wife arrived and helped also in the restaurant. With borrowed money and the knowledge of wine gained from our European background and membership in the German Wine Society. We opened the first wine lounge in Winnipeg in 1986, under the name Wine Stube. It had an impressive array of seventy-two wines from twelve countries. It was a very romantic and plush wine lounge.

Then in September 1987, Horst and his wife sold out and went back to Germany. I became sole owner of The Tea Cozy. I realized that I would be alone, and in some ways I enjoyed that, although on the other hand, it frightened me because from here on I was responsible for everything again. I had to make all the decisions for the restaurant, the staff and my private life. I missed the advice and support my brother gave at times. It had been good to have a man around.

Maria Carvalho and Linda Kindret
were with me for more then fifteen years.
Showing Biscuits and Quiche from the Tea Cozy

I tried to carry on with the Wine Stube, but for all our enthusiam, Horst and I had been ten years too early for this type of establishment in Winnipeg. Customers basked in the elegance of the space, but only consumed one or two glasses of wine, which wasn't enough to pay the rent or make up for the free samples. The long hours also made it too tedious, So, painful as it was, I had to close the Wine Stube in 1989.

In the meantime, I continued to run The Tea Cozy and kept repaying the loan on the Wine Stube. It was hard to make ends meet, and I often wondered if I would make it. I paid myself a tiny wage and Ilona and I lived on very little. I'm very grateful for the unconditional support and love Camille and my children gave whenever I asked for their assistance at The Tea Cozy, and the restaurant survived the tough times.

Both while Horst was here and later, I had many employees who were so loyal to me and we have remained good friends over the years. I even had two employees, Linda Kindret and Maria Carvalho, who were with me for more than fifteen years. They faithfully supported me through thick and thin. They are special people to me and I ensured that they were made to feel that they worked *with* me rather than *for* me. Their knowledge and assistance often inspired me. We all had so many laughs.

One employee that I took over from the former owner still stands out in my mind: Angela. She was an extraordinary young person with so much passion for all the things she did. She decided after two year of working with me to go on holiday to Italy, to the country of her immigrant parents. She met her future husband there, and has lived in Italy ever since. I was very sorry that I had to lose her but we are still in touch through all these years.

It was a matter of tremendous personal pride for me to maintain very high standards even when I was going through some difficult times. You must not think the restaurant was all fun and pleasure; much hard work had to be put into it. Sometimes I worked a sixty-five hour week, and that was not counting the extra hours at home cooking and cleaning and doing laundry, and the time I had to steal to spend with the kids and friends. Then there was all the accounting, payroll, bills to be paid and so on. Meantime, I continued to hone my own skills with courses in subjects like restaurant management, and food handling, as well as attending trade shows and continuing my own academic development.

I also was very active in the community and business community. I supported non-profit organizations like the Gas Station Theatre, I was Treasurer for five years for the Osborne Village Business Improvement Zone, and I was a member of both the Manitoba Restaurant Association and the Osborne Village Merchants' Association. I did cooking demonstrations on CKND-TV, taught healthy cooking for the Heart and Stroke Foundation, and hosted countless wine-tastings in The Tea Cozy. I was active in German Community TV and the Winnipeg Community Policing committee.

In 1998 I participated in the MacDonald's Youth Life Training Program to help young people to have the opportunity to learn work skills like cooking, and also social skills like independence and communication with others. One young woman, Jennifer, certainly achieved all that at my place. Another time I hired three troubled street kids through the Powerhouse Job Bank. They were teens who were at risk. I taught them about work, and getting along with people. I even had to teach them hygiene! I also learned that all some of these young people needed was for someone to trust them, and to know they could trust an adult. How proud I was to see those young and lost people find their way back into society after working with me. None of them ever stole from me. I trained many other young people, and I am so glad I could provide the teaching, trust, and love and the right atmosphere for them to get a fresh start.

Meanwhile, The Tea Cozy was making a name for itself. An item in the newspaper said, that "The Tea Cozy is a unique replica of an English tea house from the early part of the nineteen hundreds. It is warm and cozy and comfortable, with soft blue walls, red velour curtains and white lace tablecloths. The soft glow of the little candle-style wall lights and the background classical or light jazz mood music create nostalgia for old Europe." I was always meticulous in maintaining the tradition of High Tea in a real English tea room. We used elegant silver teapots and sugar bowls and creamers, and the Blue Willow dishes let you step back in time. Somebody said The Tea Cozy was the "quiet oasis" in busy Osborne Village. And my cooking quickly gained a great reputation! My kitchen produced homemade-style soups, quiches, crêpes and hearty Irish soda bread. We were renowned for our tea biscuits or scones which we served with Devonshire cream and strawberry preserve.

The Tea Cozy also had a very special tea cup reader, the Cameo Lady, who worked with me for 12 years, from 1982-1994, and retired at age eighty two. She had worked for the previous owner and stayed on when I bought the place. She was a woman with a lot of wisdom and she made many people who believed in her happy with her readings. She could read many people's cups without getting tired. She was often compared to Madame Red, a private reader here in Winnipeg who was well-known and had many clients. Madame Red is also now deceased. Often I was told that the Cameo Lady could tell the future, and I have often been asked, did she ever tell mine? Most of the time, I was too busy to stop for a tea-cup reading then. After the Cameo Lady retired, I had a young man called David. He had such a good sense of humour and was a very good employee. Finally, I had Madame LeFlour who was also an outstanding tea-cup reader and worked with us for some years.

If you could browse through my guestbook you would find

customers from all parts of the globe. I have been privileged to make the acquaintance of many famous people and I get gratifying postcards from afar. There is the Metropolitan Opera singer, Eva Zseller, who was in Winnipeg guest-starring in *Madame Butterfly* staged by the Manitoba Opera Association. She loved my place. Lloyd Axworthy, who was a cabinet minister in Jean Chretien's Liberal government and is now president of the University of Winnipeg, often relaxed with his family on visits to my place. Susan Thompson, who was mayor of Winnipeg from 1992 to 1998, had a very happy personality and she loved my biscuits. Glen Murray, the next mayor, also enjoyed his visits to the tea room with his mom. The writer and painter, Jackson Beardy, loved to sit quietly and sip his tea and talk with me about life. And I must not forget Mr. Ruffini, the Wine King of Italy, for whom I cooked a private meal for twenty people; and, the lovely ballerina, the quiet and shy Evelyn Hart. Many other well-known people also came to relax at The Tea Cozy, and I had many other regular customers.

One memorable day in 1986, on the day of a severe snowstorm, my Ilona and I trudged one hour through the snow to The Tea Cozy to offer free hot soup and tea to people stranded in the Village; I contacted the radio stations to let people know. What a day that was! I do not know if any one else opened on that day. I felt it was my responsibility to give my service back to the community which had given me so much.

I put my heart and soul into that restaurant, but I was rewarded. I was given the special Food Service Achievement Award by the City of Winnipeg, in recognition of five consecutive years of winning food service merit awards for exemplary performance in the food service industry. I was a very enthusiastic supporter of tourism and in 1997 and again in1999 I was awarded the "Star of the City" Award in recognition of my hospitality to visitors. There were many nominations of The Tea Cozy from a wide range of tourists.

I had the habit of drawing maps on paper napkins to direct visitors where to go, what to see and what to do. Altogether I received nine Merit Awards from the City of Winnipeg's Environment and Health Department before I retired, a feat not achieved by any other restaurant.

But Osborne Village was changing. It had started out in the late 'sixties as a few blocks south of the Osborne Bridge, where cheap apartments were available. Lots of what they called "counter-culture" people moved in, intellectuals, revolutionaries, and kids who just wanted to get high. The cheap rents in the old run-down apartment buildings also began to attract many artists and artisans. There were inexpensive eating places and small shops where the artists sold their arts and crafts. By the mid-seventies, specialty shops, boutiques and trendy restaurants began to move in, and took over what had become a flourishing, *avant-garde* neighborhood district. The shops and apartments were renovated, and many successful businesses sprang up. When I first had The Tea Cozy, there were places like Morning Star Clothing, Mannequin Clothing, Male Ego Men's Wear, restaurants like The Beefeater, Pasquale's, and Engel's. Between the bridge and Corydon Avenue there were also a number of independent businesses like Dutch Maid Ice Cream, Moxley Rentals, Floating Ecstasy (a water-bed store) and the Humbug Christmas Store. DesArt sold fine art and David Rice made beautiful and expensive jewelry that he sold in his store. There was the famous Happy Cooker, and of course, Basil's and Swallows. Many of the businesses are still there; others have changed owners or new businesses have moved in. In the 'eighties, I was very proud to be one of the young, bright-eyed entrepreneurs who were out every morning sweeping the sidewalks in front of our shops and greeting and chatting with each other.

But the Village continued to evolve through the 'eighties, and I needed a strong back to survive the changes that started to take place. Other areas were copying the success of Osborne Village and the focus shifted away to places like The Forks, Academy Road, and Corydon Avenue, where trendy restaurants and specialty shops were opening. Then the panhandlers, street kids and squeegee kids came more and more to the Village, and as South Winnipeg grew, traffic became very heavy. We all did what we could to cope with the changes. Many merchants redesigned their places of business to keep up with the times. I kept my customers coming with what The Tea Cozy had always offered: great food and good service in the atmosphere of a traditional English tea room. I also employed many musicians to play there, like Leslie McInnis (harp), Eric Lussier (harpsichord), June "Pepper" Harris (piano and vocals), Dana Starkell (classical guitar), and Ruth Lindemeir (Zither). Many artists boosted their careers by performing at The Tea Cozy.

The highlight of my career as owner of The Tea Cozy was to receive the 2000 Manitoba Woman Entrepreneur of the Year Award for Lifetime Achievement. I was nominated by a former employee, a wonderful young woman named Charlotte Crossman. Several women were nominated every year, but only twelve were chosen to be finalists. This recognition of my hard work and community spirit and business sense gave me great satisfaction and I was delighted to be nominated.

The Awards Banquet of the Women Business Owners of Manitoba for 2000 was held May 12 at the Holiday Inn Downtown. My three children and my husband and all of my employees were there on that special day. A woman bagpiper marched the nominees into a room filled with six hundred guests, and warm applause welcomed us. But I did not think I would win. There were twelve women nominated for awards, but only five awards. As it came time to hand out the final award, the Lifetime Achievement one, I was called up and I was so surprised and shocked that I left the speech I had written, just in case I was chosen, on the table. For that reason my speech was very short, and the Free Press chose it the next day as the "Quote of the Day" under my photo:

Women Business Owners of Manitoba Winner
Roswitha Scharf-Dessureault
of the Tea Cozy Restaurant, lifetime achievement.

And there wasn't a dry eye in the place when Roswitha accepted her award:
"Such a moment, it's like a moment of love, to be remembered."

I could see even then, though, that the time was coming when I must give up the life I had built over twenty years for myself and my employees at The Tea Cozy. First it began that many of my older customers could no longer get up the stairs, and to attract the younger generation I would have had to make drastic changes to the restaurant. I was not willing to do that. And then we had three break-ins within two years. One time they came up the back staircase, broke through the glass door, and destroyed my office and I had to sit all night to wait to have the door covered up with wood. Another time, I got a call to go to the restaurant late at night. When I arrived, shivering and scared, the police officer who had called told me that a man had been hallucinating that he was out hunting. He had smashed the front door and dropped a handful of high-power rifle shells. From then on, every time I received a call from the alarm system company at night, I feared the worst. Also, sometimes I came very early to work and someone would be asleep at the front door of the restaurant. I would have to call the police to remove that person.

We had a small party for Camille on his sixtieth birthday at The Tea Cozy on November 23, 1999. That night after we had gone home, I received a call from the fire department that Osborne would be closed from Stradbrook to River Avenues because of a huge fire across the street that destroyed four businesses near the corner of Osborne and Stradbrook, including The Happy Cooker. My husband and I went in that early morning and the smell of smoldering ashes and smoke that stung the eyes was everywhere, even in the restaurant. We had to close for three days. Some of my employees came in early that morning to film the fire in the Village. It was arson! It was a shock for me and I made up my mind there and then to sell the restaurant before anything worse happened.

And so I sold The Tea Cozy on January 7, 2002. An article in the *Free Press* said, "It's an end of an era -- after two decades in Osborne Village The Tea Cozy Restaurant will be no more". But it was not that easy as I thought it would be when the day came to hand over The Tea Cozy, later that month. I made one more time my rounds in the restaurant and made sure that everything was clean and orderly. On that day I was alone, and I could have washed the whole restaurant with my tears. I could hardly control myself as I said farewell to my life of twenty years at the restaurant. But as I closed the door for the last time, I was full of memories, good and bad, about my business, my employees and customers, and Osborne Village. These memories will stay with me for the rest of my life. Still, I needed over two years to really realize that The Tea Cozy was gone and no longer my life. I often think of my life in The Tea Cozy, and I can still almost hear the chatter and laughter I had with the customers. It was a joyful and fulfilling time, even through all the many hours of hard work. Financially, though, the sale of the restaurant did not leave very much for my retirement, so I still must work part-time. I continue to teach at the *Kinderschule* and the children continue to bless me with their innocence and light.

Over the summer when there is no *Kinderschule*, I am employed by Fehr-Way Tours as a tour director for day trips and a few longer trips, where I can use my experience and knowledge of the hospitality industry. My trips take me all around Manitoba and north-western Ontario, and I have to research the various destinations so I can tell the passengers about them. Among my favorite are: the Wild Rose Tour to Roseisle; the Archibald Museum in Pembina, which celebrates the life of Nellie McClung, a very important leader in the fight to get votes for women early in the last century; and the tour to the Rose Lane Heritage House and Tea Room. I have also enjoyed guiding the tours to the Six Pines Ranch (a farm), and the trips to Gimli, Riding Mountain National Park, Lake of the Woods, the International Peace Garden and the Honey and Garlic Festival in Manitou. I very much enjoyed the trip to Sioux Narrows; and, the seven-day tour of the Agawa Canyon & Mackinac Island. This summer I have guided a ten-day tour called *"Amish Country Flavour"* which took us from Wisconsin Dells to Chicago, Illinois, and then through Indiana's and Ohio's Amish communities.

The tourists are mostly seniors, like me, and each summer I see many of the old customers who had travelled with me the year before. How happy we are to see each other again! I have made friends with some of the regular ladies, and we go together for coffee and talk. As I take the seniors on the bus trips, I become an entertainer and master of ceremonies. We play bingo, sing songs, do puzzles, and I make jokes with them until we reach our destination. There I look after them by making sure about their meals and their safety, as well as showing them around. The seniors love to laugh and really enjoy our times together. Sometimes my pronunciation gets in the way of what I am trying to explain to them, and so I tell them a couple of funny stories about my mistakes with English. One time, for example, while I still ran The Tea Cozy, I did a TV cooking show on CKND, demonstrating my Irish Soda Bread. As I was going through the required ingredients, I explained that in this bread there was "no conservative." The camera man began to laugh, and the host got a very surprised look on her face, but I didn't understand why. I did not realize my mistake until the show was over and the host explained what I had said and what I had really meant. They found it especially funny because there was an election coming up. Even after many years of learning English I still did not understand the difference between "preservative" and "conservative". Some time later my husband mentioned this incident to Lloyd Axworthy, a staunch Liberal, who replied: "I'll buy that!". Another time I had gone to visit some friends, and when I knocked on their door, they both answered it in their dressing gowns. I was startled and a bit embarrassed, and I said, "Oh, I'm so sorry! I didn't mean to destroy you!" Of course, what I meant to say was "disturb you," not "destroy." My friends still chuckle when they recall my mistake. And the people in the bus have a great laugh when I tell them these stories. But they know then that I don't take myself so seriously, and when I make mistakes, we all laugh and then they correct my pronunciation,

It gives me a lot of pleasure to help my seniors enjoy their trips across the Manitoba prairies and into the Laurentian Shield of northern Ontario to see the beauty of our country. And my time with the seniors balances very beautifully my time with the little kindergarteners. The children keep me young and curious, and from my seniors I see and learn how to live a happy and healthy old age.

If somebody were to ask me what I've learned from my many travels and adventures, bad times and good times, I would say "Never stop learning and never be afraid to try something new. People are born with many strengths and talents, but if you don't test yourself, you never find out what they are." There is a passage by Marianne Williamson which

I love very much. It is called *Our Deepest Fear* and it says for me what I have learned on my journeys:

Our deepest fear is not that we are inadequate.
Our deepest fear is that we are powerful beyond measure.
It is our light, not our darkness
That most frightens us.

We ask ourselves
Who am I to be brilliant, gorgeous, talented, fabulous?
Actually, who are you not to be?
You are a child of God.

Your playing small
Does not serve the world.
There's nothing enlightened about shrinking
So that other people won't feel insecure around you.

We are all meant to shine,
As children do.
We were born to make manifest
The glory of God that is within us.

It's not just in some of us;
It's in everyone.

And as we let our own light shine,
We unconsciously give other people permission to do the same.
As we're liberated from our own fear,
Our presence automatically liberates others.

[**Note:** This inspiring quote is taken from Marianne Williamson's book *A Return to Love*. Though often quoted as part of Nelson Mandela's moving speech when he was inaugurated as South Africa's first black president, it does not appear in the speech.]

You never know who you can become until you try. Doors will open and close in life, and opportunities will come and go. Know yourself and use your gifts and you will be able to climb mountains -- even if you have to kick yourself.

And sometimes, if you're lucky, maybe God gives you a kick also!

APPENDICES

THE TEA COZY'S FAVORITE RECIPES

THE TEA COZY RECIPES

Here are some of the most popular recipes that my customers have repeatedly requested.
Have fun cooking, and enjoy the food!

THE TEA COZY GINGERBREAD

1 ½	cup	sugar
1 ½	teaspoon	cinnamon
4 ½	teaspoons	ginger
1	teaspoon	salt
3 ¾	cup	flour
1 ½	cup	vegetable Oil
1	can	apple sauce (add 200ml of water)
1	cup	molasses (blackstrap)
1	cup	honey, or Corn Syrup
3		eggs
1	cup	boiling water
3	teaspoons	baking soda

Method:

Place the first 10 ingredients in a large bowl. Mix and blend thoroughly. Add one can of apple sauce, one cup of water. Mix baking soda into the boiling water and gradually add to the mixture. Blend well. Pour batter into a greased 9"x13" pan, lined with wax paper. Bake in oven at 350°F for 1 ¼ hour, or until a pick inserted into the center comes out clean. Cool in pan.

Serve hot, with whipped cream.

Serves 12

Tea Cozy Tea Biscuits

2/3   cup margarine
¼   cup sugar
8   cups flour
1   teaspoon salt
16   teaspoon baking powder
2   eggs
4 ½   cup milk

Method:
Rub 2/3 cup of margarine into flour until well mixed. Beat the 2 eggs slightly and mix with 4 ½ cup milk, add milk and eggs mixture to margarine and flour.
The dough must be well mixed because it is not kneaded. Put dough out on well floured surface and pat down to a uniform thickness. Brush top of biscuits with an egg wash

Bake biscuit at 450° for 10 – 15 minutes.
Makes: 28 Biscuits

"Serve two tea biscuit per person with strawberry jam and Devonshire, or clotted cream.

What is clotted cream ?

Clotted cream is obtained by heating unpasturized milk until the cream separates and floats to the surface. The thick cream is then removed and used. This clotted cream is, classically, spread on scones or served along side fresh fruit.
Clotted cream is a classic component of English tea service. Another name for clotted cream is Devonshire cream, as that is the region in England where this cream is considered a delicacy. This will last up to four days if refrigerated in a tightly sealed container.

TEA COZY TRIFLE PUDDING

1   layer sponge cake
1   cup sherry
4   cups fresh strawberries
2   cups whipped cream
4 ½ cups vanilla pudding

Method:
Break sponge cake into 1 inch cubes.
Pour sherry over cake to soak.
In a large bowl, layer cake, fruit, and custard.
Garnish with whipped cream.

Note: During the Christmas season, mincemeat can be used instead of fresh fruit

Maria's Bread Pudding

½ loaf bread, (sandwich loaf / white or brown)
¼ cup white sugar
¼ cup brown sugar
2 tablespoon lemon juice
1 egg
½ cup water
½ cup milk
½ cup raisins
1 teaspoon cinnamon

Method:
All ingredients into one large bowl. Grease an 8 x11 baking pan, Fill with mix Top with cinnamon.
Bake 20-30 minutes at 300°

Serve hot with whipped cream, Serves 6

TEA COZY APPLE CAKE

2   cups margarine
2   cups sugar
4   eggs
4   cups flour
2   teaspoons baking powder
1   teaspoon baking soda
2   cups milk
6   apples (each sliced into 6 wedges)
½   cup brown sugar
6   teaspoons cinnamon

Method:
Beat butter and sugar well. add eggs, one at a time, beating well after each addition.
together: flour, baking powder and baking soda.
Add flour mixture to margarine mixture, alternately with the milk, beginning and ending with flour.

Pour batter into a greased 9x13" pan, lined with wax paper.

Arrange apple wedges to cover entire surface. Sprinkle brown sugar and cinnamon evenly over apples.
Place in 350°F oven. Bake 1½ hour. Insert a toothpick in center of cake; it has to come out clean.

Cool in pan. May be served hot with whipped cream.
Serves: 12

TEA COZY IRISH SODA BREAD

3   cups whole wheat flour
3   cups white flour
¾   cup margarine
5   tablespoons baking powder
2   teaspoons baking soda
½   teaspoon salt
1   tablespoon sugar
3   cups buttermilk

Method:
Mix dry ingredients, rub in soft margarine, add buttermilk.
Knead at least for 20 strokes. Press into 9 inch round cake tins.
Score top of loaves with an "X". Dust with flour.
Let rise at least 10 minutes. Bake at 350°F for 35 minutes.

Makes 3 loaves of delicious bread.

HONEY GINGERBREAD (20 PIECES) FOR CHRISTMAS TIME

1   cup of margarine
2   cups honey
1   cup sugar (fine white)
1   teaspoon cinnamon
1   teaspoon ginger
1   teaspoon nutmeg
1   teaspoon clove
2   teaspoons cocoa
7   cups flour
2   teaspoons baking powder
¼   teaspoon salt
2   eggs

Method:
Melt margarine in saucepan over low heat. Add: honey, sugar, spices and cocoa. Stir until sugar has dissolved. Cool mixture. In a large bowl sift together flour, baking powder and salt. Add eggs and cooled mixture and knead until smooth. Divide dough into thirds and roll out dough.

Cut out gingerbread man ½ to ¾ inch thick and bake at 350° F (180°C) for 15 minutes or until done.

German Plumcake

125 grams	butter
¾ cup	sugar
6	eggs
1 lb	white flour
6 teaspoons	baking powder
¾ cup	milk
4 lb	blue plums
½ lb	flour
75 grams	butter
75 grams	sugar
1 teaspoon	vanilla extract

Method:
Mix Butter and sugar well. Slowly add the eggs to it. Mix white flour with baking powder. Add milk then pour the batter into a 17½ x11½" flat floured cookie sheet.
Slice plums into 4 wedges and lay on top of batter.

Crumb Mixture:
Flour, sugar, vanilla extract and butter. Sprinkle loosely on top of the plums.
Bake at 375°F for 40 minutes.

TEA COZY ASPARAGUS ROLLS

8 slices   bread (toasted)
1 can   asparagus Tips or fresh asparagus spears
100 grams   cheddar cheese

Method:
Toast white or brown bread. Trim the crusts off after toasted. Place shaved cheddar cheese in the middle, then asparagus spears. Close with a toothpick and add more cheddar cheese on top.

Microwave for 3 minutes or in toaster oven.

Serve hot with salad. Serves 2

Red Cabbage

5   lbs red cabbage
1   tablespoon margarine
2   apples
1   onion
2   bay leaves
    salt / pepper
½   teaspoon clove
1½ - 2 cups red wine
1   cup of water
2   tablespoons brown sugar
3   teaspoons red wine vinegar

Method:
1 big head of red cabbage cut small into a large pot. Sauté the cabbage with olive oil or (margarine).

Add apples (cut in four). Add onion, bay leaves, clove, salt & pepper, brown sugar. Mix well. Add 1½ cup red wine (or water) and let cook on medium heat for 1 to 1½ hour; turn it once in a while and add a little water as required. Let it simmer. Before serving, remove the bay leaves and add 2 teaspoons of red wine vinegar. Gently mix the vinegar into the cabbage and serve hot.
The vinegar brings back the rich red color of the red cabbage. Enjoy.
Serves 8 Persons

Rouladen (Braised Stuffed Beef Rolls)

Old German recipe

1 lb boneless top round beef (baron of beef), cut very thin (about 1/4" slices)
mustard, salt and pepper, sweet paprika
1 slice medium sliced bacon (not too thick)
onion wedge and ½ a pickle sliced lengthwise
butter (or margarine), for browning the meat
¾ cup red wine, or beef broth or water
flour (or rice flour)

Method:
Have the butcher slice the beef into thin slices, figuring 1-2 slices per person. Spread them out on the counter and spread them evenly with good quality mustard and sweet paprika, salt & pepper. Lay slice of bacon, the onion wedge and the pickle on the meat. Roll up firmly and tuck the ends in securely with toothpicks (or white thread). Make sure none of the ingredients can fall out!

Brown the pieces on all sides in a skillet with some olive oil or butter (or margarine).

Add the wine or broth or water; cover, and simmer gently at 375°F for about 45 to 60 minutes. Remove the rolls to a platter. Whisk-in enough flour (or rice flour), salt & pepper to the skillet to make a smooth gravy.
Season with salt & pepper and serve.
Enjoy! Serves 4 Persons

CRÊPES BATTER

6   eggs
¼ cup oil
½ cup flour
½ cup rice flour
1¼ cup 1% low–fat milk

Mix well; add a pinch of salt and sugar.
In a pan, fry each side 1 min, using canola oil.
The crêpes must turn out paper thin.

Crêpe Filling (as Desired)

Method:
In saucepan,sautéed onions, garlic in 1 teaspoon of
canola oil. Add: magi seasoning (spiced seasoning from
Switzerland). Add: fresh mushroom & cooked chicken; add
a tablespoon of chicken broth; add ½ cup of rice flour. Let
simmer for 5-8 minutes.
Spread filling onto crêpe. Roll and serve with melted
mozzarella cheese on top.

Serve crêpe with a variety of garden salad.

Asparagus "Variety of Quiche & Egg Batter"

7   eggs
1   cup 1% low–fat milk
¼   cup whipped cream
400 grams mozzarella or cheddar cheese
1/3 teaspoon pepper
     pinch of salt

Method:
Line a quiche pan with rolled–out pastry. Drain 1 can asparagus, sprinkle on bottom of pan, top with 400 grams cheddar or mozzarella cheese. Then pour cream & egg mixture on top. Sprinkle with dried parsley flakes or dill.

Place avocado slice on top. Bake at 350°F for 1½ hour. Cool before serving.

AVOCADO & CRAB QUICHE

1 whole avocado
1 can crab meat
400 grams cheddar (or mozzarella) cheese
    pinch salt & pepper

Method:
Line a quiche pan with rolled–out pastry; cut slice of
avocado on top of pastry; drain 1 can crabmeat sprinkle
on avocado; top with 400 grams of cheddar or mozzarella
cheese. Then pour cream & egg mixture on top. Sprinkle
with dried parsley flakes or dill.

Place avocado slice on top. Bake at 350° for 1 ½ hour.

Cool before serving.

SUGGESTIONS FOR A VARIETY OF QUICHES

Bacon & Tomato Quiche

Spinach & Cottage Cheese Quiche

Spinach & Feta Quiche

Wild Rice & Turkey Breast Quiche

Asparagus Quiche

Crab & Shrimp Quiche

Quiche Lorraine (Ham)

Vegetarian Quiche

Mushroom & Chicken Quiche

Greek Quiche (Feta cheese green & red pepper-onions & green olives)

Artichoke & Pimento Quiche

Spinach & Mushroom Quiche

All Vegetables must be steamed or Sautéed before baking.

Each Quiche serves 7 people.

EIERSTICH (EGGDROP) SOUP

Ingredients:

¼   cup flour
2   eggs
3   tablepoons milk
    salt & pepper
1 or 2 strands green onion

4   cups water for the stock (¼ chicken - or can of chicken broth)

Stock: First, prepare the chicken stock. Boil the chicken in 4 cups of water; remove chicken; and, add green onions. or use chicken broth

Method:
Eggdrop: Mix the eggs into 3 tablespoons of milk; add flour; salt & pepper.
Dip a teaspoon into hot water; scoop out a ¼ teaspoon of batter and let it drip into the boiling chicken stock. The drippings will form the little egg drops; they sink to the bottom at first and when they are ready they float to the top. You can stir-in some finely chopped fresh parsley into the batter. It can also be sprinkled on top of the soup.

Serve very Hot / Serves 4 people

Beer & Cheddar Cheese Soup

8   ounces black ale beer (1 bottle)
2   small onions
2   pounds mild cheddar cheese
¼   cup of flour
¼   cup milk
4   liter chicken stock
1   pinch salt
1   pinch pepper
1   pinch nutmeg
1   cup margarine

Method:
Melt margarine with onions, salt & pepper. Then, add chicken stock. Mix the milk & flour and stir into the stock. Let it come to a boil then remove from heat and wisk-in the cheddar cheese and keep wisking until melted.

Wisk at all times, until the soup thickens. Add: nutmeg and ale beer. Move the cook pot aside as the beer will bubble up; stir slowly until the bubbles subside.

Serve with fresh chopped parsley or a dash of nutmeg on top. It is a delicious Soup

CREAM OF CARROT SOUP

2	tablespoons margarine (canola)
3	potatoes
24	carrots
3	cloves garlic
3	tablespoons brown sugar
1	teaspoon dill
1	cup milk
1½	cup chicken stock
¼	cup white flour/ or rice flour
	pinch salt
	pinch pepper

Method:

Melt margarine in a saucepan; add vegetables, salt &
pepper and brown sugar. Sauté, then add chicken broth.
Cover and cook until vegetables are very tender. Stir-in
unsweetened rice flour and milk.

Bring soup to a boil; reduce heat and let simmer for 20-30
minutes.

Remove from heat, mix with hand blender; add green
onions and fresh chopped parsley as you serve it.

CREAM OF POTATO SOUP

8 medium potatoes
1 onions chopped
1 stalk green onions
2 cups chicken broth
1 teaspoon salt
1 cup milk
1 cup heavy cream
2 teaspoons margarine
2 teaspoons fresh parsley, (fine chopped)
½ teaspoon pepper
½ cup rice flour / or white flour

Method:
Melt margarine in a saucepan; add: potatoes, onions, salt &
pepper; and sauté"
Then add chicken broth. Cover and cook until potatoes are
very tender.
Bring soup to a boil, reduce heat and let simmer for 20–30
minutes.
Stir-in unsweetened rice flour with milk and heavy
cream; let simmer for 5 more minutes
then add green onions.

Mix with hand blender; add fresh chopped parsley as you
serve it. (HOT)

Serves 6

PHOTOS & DOCUMENTS

Roswitha Scharf-Dessureault of the Tea Cozy Restaurant.
Winner of the 2000 Women Business Owners of Manitoba,
Lifetime Achievement

Wunderbar! Very Elegant and Serene
settings.
Sumptous Desserts and
Excellent Friendly Service
Thankyou + Blessings Rose - Marie,
Hawaii

Truly delicious Elaine

Wonderful, Warm & Friendly...
As Always, Thank You Rose,
Dicindy

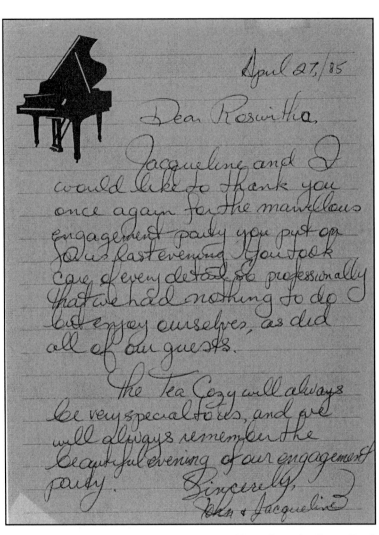

April 27,/85

Dear Roswitha,

Jacqueline and I would like to thank you once again for the marvellous engagement party you put on for us last evening. You took care of every detail so professionally that we had nothing to do but enjoy ourselves, as did all of our guests.

The Tea Cozy will always be very special to us, and we will always remember the beautiful evening of our engagement party.

Sincerely,
John & Jacqueline

Notes from the Guest Book

Receiving "Star of the City" Award 1987
from Mayor Susan Thompson

Receiving "Star of the City" Award 1999
From Mayor Glen Murray

164

SUSAN A. THOMPSON
MAYOR • MAIRE • ALCALDESA

CITY OF WINNIPEG
CITY HALL
510 MAIN STREET
WINNIPEG, MANITOBA
R3B 1B9
(204) 986-2196
FAX: (204) 949-0566

VILLE DE WINNIPEG
HÔTEL DE VILLE
510, RUE MAIN
WINNIPEG (MANITOBA)
R3B 1B9
(204) 986-2196
TÉLÉC. : (204) 949-0566

CIUDAD DE WINNIPEG
MUNICIPALIDAD
510 MAIN STREET
WINNIPEG, MANITOBA
R3B 1B9
(204) 986-2196
FAX. (204) 949-0566

October 1, 1997

Ms. Roswitha Scharf-Dessureault
The Tea Cozy
Winnipeg, Manitoba

Dear Ms. Scharf-Dessureault:

I would like to take this opportunity to say "Congratulations!" on your nomination as a "Stars of the City" Hospitality Ambassador.

This program recognizes individuals and organizations who have gone out of their way to provide outstanding hospitality to travellers. Nominations were received from tourists travelling from all over the globe. We all play an important role in attracting tourism to Winnipeg and from the time tourists arrive until the time they depart, it is the friendly and hospitable service which Winnipeg is known for, which keeps our visitors returning year after year. It is only through the continued efforts of individuals such as yourselves that Winnipeg will continue to be known as the - "One Great City" around the world.

Once again, my sincerest "Congratulations" and Thank You for playing your part in making this City an exceptional place to visit.

Yours very truly,

Susan A. Thompson,
MAYOR.

WINNIPEG - HOST CITY OF THE 1999 PAN AM GAMES
WINNIPEG - VILLE HÔTESSE DES JEUX PANAMÉRICAINS DE 1999
WINNIPEG - CIUDAD ANFITRIONA DE LOS JUEGOS PANAMERICANOS DE 1999

October 1, 1997
Letter from Mayor Susan Thompson

MANITOBA

LEGISLATIVE ASSEMBLY

Room 172
Leader of the Opposition

August 26, 1988

Ms. Roswitha Ingrid Scharf
833 Grosvenor Avenue
Winnipeg, Manitoba
R3M 0M3

Dear Ms. Roswitha Ingrid Scharf:

I am delighted to welcome you to the family of Canadaian citizens. Canada and Manitoba are fortunate that you have chosen to live among us and to participate fully in our political, social and economic life.

As your Member of the Legislative Assembly for River Heights, I hope that you will contact me if you have questions or problems with your provincial government. Do not hesitate to call me at my office at the Legislature, 945-3712 or to write to me at Room 172, 450 Broadway, Winnipeg, Manitoba, M.B. R3C 0V8.

Enjoy your citzenship with all the rights and responsibilites it brings with it.

Sincerely,

Sharon Carstairs

Sharon Carstairs, MLA
Leader, Liberal Party in Manitoba

August 26, 1988
Letter from Sharon Carstairs, MLA

Hon. Lloyd Axworthy, PC, MP
Winnipeg South Centre
418-N
House of Commons
Ottawa, ON
K1A 0A6
Tel: 613-996-0163
Fax: 613-947-6542

Constituency Office
445 Stradbrook Avenue
Winnipeg, MB
R3L 0J2
Tel: 204-983-3290
Fax: 204-983-3236

May 10, 2000

Roswitha Scharf-Dessureault
The Tea Cozy
303-99 Osborne St.
Winnipeg, MB
R3L 2R4

Dear Roswitha,

It was with great pleasure that I read in Monday's Winnipeg Sun the article recognizing your achievements and your nomination for the Woman Entrepreneur of the Year award. I would like to offer you my congratulations. As a longstanding customer of The Tea Cozy, I have always enjoyed your warm hospitality and delicious food. I look forward to dropping in for lunch sometime soon.

Best regards,

Lloyd Axworthy, MP
Winnipeg South Centre

May 10, 2000
Letter from Hon. Lloyd Axworthy, MP

THE CITY OF WINNIPEG

COUNCILLORS' OFFICE

CIVIC CENTRE • 510 MAIN STREET • WINNIPEG • MANITOBA • R3B 1B9

JENNY GERBASI
Councillor
FORT ROUGE WARD
City-Centre Community
Committee

Telephone: 986-5878
Fax: 986-5636

December 20, 2001

Ms Roswitha Scharf-Dessureault
The Tea Cozy
303-99 Osborne Street
Winnipeg, MB   R3L 1Y4

Dear Roswitha,

It has come to my attention that you will be retiring at the end of 2001 and that the Tea Cozy will be no more.

First, I want to congratulate you on your incredible success you have had for so many years with this wonderful establishment.

I have to say it is going to seem very strange not to have the TeaCozy any more in Osborne Village and it is a great loss.

However, you have served our community so well and for so long that there is no excuse for begrudging you a peaceful and relaxing retirement and the opportunity to devote your time to other things.

On behalf of the constituents of Fort Rouge, I would like to thank you profoundly for all you have given to this city. I will make every effort to get to the Tea Cozy to see you before it serves its last piece of gingerbread.

With warm and sincere best wishes,

Jenny Gerbasi
Jenny Gerbasi
Councillor
Fort Rouge Ward

Embrace the Spirit • Vivez l'esprit

December 20, 2001
Letter from Councillor Jenny Gerbasi, Fort Rouge Ward

CANADIAN IMMIGRANT'S RECORD CARD
CARD NO. 138
s.s. MAASDAM
HOLLAND-AMERICA LINE
ROTTERDAM-QUEBEC
21 SEP 1967

Canadian Immigration Record Card Number 138

Wappen
der Familie Nothnagel um 1600

1600 Nothnagel Family Crest

*_NOTHNAGEL_*
* *

FAMILY HISTORY
* *

The name *Nothnagel* goes back to at least 1413, in Hildburghausen, a town in the district of Thuringen, Germany. *Claus Nothnagel* appears as a gentleman / Radherr/ or gentleman advisor. During the Thirty Years War (1618-1648), a *Jacob Nothnagel *went to Darmstadt, probably to the Lichtenberg Castle. Two of his sons settled down as citizens of Griesheim, and *Johannes Nothnagel* is our direct ancestor.

On September 20, 1809, *Phillip Karl Nothnagel II* was born in Griesheim. He married /Josephine Katherine Weber/, also born in Griesheim (May 5, 1838). They are my great-great grandparents. Phillip died in Darmstadt on November 1, 1909, and Josephine on October 5, 1909.

My great grandparents were *Phillip Karl Nothnagel III, *born November 24, 1886 in Griesheim, and *Katharina Stauder*, born February 2, 1862 in Griesheim. I don't know their dates of death. They had four children:

Heinrich Q. (September 9,1885 – January 20,1973)
Konrad (June 3,1888 – August 1, 1889)
Katharine (May 1,1893 - ?)
*Elisabethe *(July 18, 1893 – March 27, 1942).

My other great-grandparents on my mother's side were *Adam Walter* and *Margareta Lutz*, whose dates I don't know. Their son, *Adam Walter Jr. *was born July 20, 1879.

Elisabethe Nothnagel, my grandmother, married my grandfather, Adam Walter* * on 23/02/1908. They lived in Darmstadt and had five children, including Mathilde, my mother:

Katharina, aka "Katie" (dates unknown)
Sebastian (October 21,1909 - ??,1991)
*Mathilde *(October 25,1912 – October 8,1962)
Adam (September 6,1914 – November 18,1985)
Karlman (December 24,1943 -)

My mother married three times:

1) to my father, Heinrich Fiedler on December 15, 1939
2) on July 8,1944 to a man whose name she never told us,
3) to Leon Feraru (February 2,1893 – August 30,1962),
father of my half-brothers, Peter, Aurel and Florel

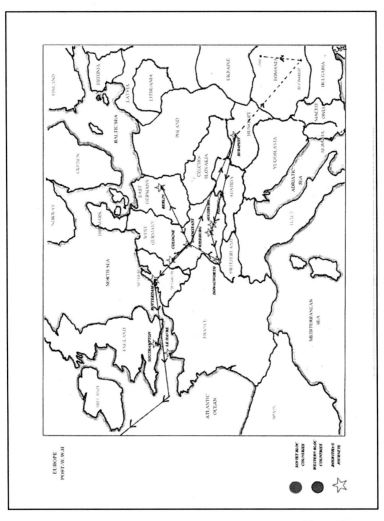

Map of Europe
Roswitha's Journey